Tom Flynn

Medium & Healer

Other books

by Sharon S. Darrow

Bottlekatz,

A Complete Care Guide for Orphan Kittens

Faces of Rescue:

Cats, Kittens & Great Danes

From Hindsight to Insight,

A Traditional to Metaphysical Memoir

Coming soon,

Laura's Dash Series:

She Survives

Desperate Choices

Her Triumph

TOM FLYNN

Medium & Healer

Tom Flynn

and

Sharon S. Darrow

Samati Press
Sacramento, California

iii

Cover Photo courtesy of Kris Machalica
Photo of Tom with drawing of Dr. Eisenberg,
    courtesy of Vivienne Brocklehurst
Photo of Tom with Kris Machalica,
    courtesy of Kris Machalica
Photo of Tom at Central Spiritualist Church,
    courtesy of Kris Machalica

Multiple published articles from the Psychic News,
courtesy of the Psychic News

First Edition 2016
ISBN-13: 978-0-9977005-3-4   (Print version)
ISBN-10: 0-9977005-3-X   (Digital versions)
ISBN-13: 978-0-9977005-6-5   (Audio version)

Library of Congress Control Number: 2016958966

Publisher: Samati Press
            Sacramento, California
Manufactured in the United States of America

Dedication

To my parents,

Dennis and Genty Flynn,

for the gifts they passed on to me,

and for continuing to support me in spirit.

Love always,

Tom

Contents

Acknowledgments
Introduction

Part One,
Tom's Story, Tom's Words

The Carpenter & The Gypsy   3

Coming of Age   11

At the Front of the Church   19

Spreading His Wings   25

Mediums & Healers   33

Stonehenge   39

London to Chesterfield   45

New Horizons, Old Memories   53

Spain & Australia   63

Malaysia, Pain & Blessings   69

Chesterfield to Ireland   75

Irish Connections   85

Kindred Spirits   91

America   99

Instrument of Love   111

Part Two,
More About Tom
by Sharon S. Darrow

Kris Machalica   115

Teresa Klimek   123

Spiritualism   127

Karen Zeppa   131

Barbara   141

David M. Baker   145

Vivienne Brocklehurst   149

Newspaper Articles   153

Psychic News   167

Conclusion   177

Resources   179

Acknowledgments

Special thanks to my family members for all their love and support throughout my life, and to my mom and dad who continue to help me from the spirit world.

I also need to thank Valerie, for her help in making this book possible, to Nancy who put my words on paper, to Kris for more things than I can list, and for all my other friends for their support and encouragement.

Many thanks to all the wonderful pastors and people of the Spiritualist Churches in Ireland, England, the United States and around the world for letting me participate in their services, and always making me feel welcome.

Special thanks to Sharon, who put this book together.

Tom Flynn

Acknowledgments

Special thanks to my family members for their faith in me and their encouragement.

Thank you Kris, for having the courage and determination to venture out on a rainy night to try and find someone to help with Tom's project. Without you, it wouldn't have been possible.

Thank you Norma Jean Thornton for your gracious help under an impossible deadline.

Thank you Tom for sharing your life and your vision with me. Working with you has been a joy, and I'll always treasure our friendship.

Sharon S Darrow

Introduction

What do you think of when you hear about a medium? Some people imagine a tall, cadaverous man wearing a sparkly turban in a dark room, speaking in a spooky voice about "Your dear, departed loved ones." Perhaps what comes to mind is a slick television star who entertains onscreen, and offers private readings or classes for huge fees. Other people think all mediums are scammers, fakers who tell outrageous stories and make big promises in return for large sums of cash -- "Payable in advance, please."

The vast majority of mediums, however, are ordinary people who share their amazing gifts because they're called on to do so.

Tom Flynn, an internationally known medium, is neither rich nor highly educated, nor is he traditionally religious. He's traveled throughout the world, living and sharing a powerful message about how love transcends death. He lives a simple life of faith, trusting the people he meets who invite him to speak, and the spirit guides who open doors for him whenever he needs them.

Part One

Tom's Story,
Tom's Words

The Carpenter & The Gypsy

My parents both died while when I was young, but are still with me as spirit guides from the other side. They were a most unlikely pair when they were alive, but their profound love for one another and for me continues today from the spirit world.

My mom, Gentillia, known as Genty, met my dad, Dennis Flynn, in a local pub. It didn't take long for them to fall in love in spite of their many differences.

Dennis was a strong, kind and gentle man, born of staunch Roman Catholic parents. Genty was tiny, less than five feet tall, pretty and slender, of Romany Gypsy stock. Her charismatic charm attracted the attention of every man in the room, in spite of her physical disabilities. Genty was partially paralyzed on her left side from birth, but never let that keep her from living a full life.

Falling in love and proposing to Genty was a huge risk for my dad because of his family's religious beliefs. He married her anyway, and was disowned for marrying outside of their faith.

Every Christmas my dad would send Christmas cards to the members of his family, hoping against hope that they could reconcile, but he never heard back from them because he'd married "The gypsy."

My brothers and sisters and I never got to know Dad's family, and had no idea what we were missing, especially since Mom's family spent lots of time at our house.

We lived in a two story, three bedroom council house, on Strawberry Road in Edmonton, a little village north of London. I was born on April 21, 1956, the youngest child of seven.

Genty gave birth to all of us at home, because she believed in letting her children come naturally, without hospitals or modern medicine. When my oldest brother, Michael, was born, he was so small that Mom put him in a shoebox.

My three older sisters and three older brothers, our parents, and a lodger called Jock, filled the little house to the rafters. The three girls shared a bedroom and slept together in a single bed. The boys did the same, so when I was old enough to join them, there were four of us sharing a bed.

Mom and Dad had the third bedroom, while Jock, the boarder, had a small back room on the first floor. Before I came along,

Jock had lived with my parents for years, working at odd jobs to help pay the rent, and also helping care for Genty when she needed it.

Ten people lived in our house, with no inside bathroom and no hot water, a hard life. Since all the other families in the neighborhood had the same standard of living, we didn't think of ourselves as poor. Large families were the norm, which meant I always had lots of friends to play with on the streets.

When I was around five years old, I invited about ten little boys and girls into the garden. One of my older brothers put a sheet over the line for a curtain and directed all the children to sit in front of it.

I pulled the curtain open, stepped out in my Beatles wig, and sang to everyone. I loved singing, and knew all the words to songs by Freddie and the Dreamers, the Dave Clark Five, and The Monkeys. My sister, Phyllis, played an old banjo, and together we drove everyone in the house crazy, especially our parents.

Genty and Dennis doted on us children, but my dad had to handle most of the physical chores because of Mom's health. He did the cooking, and would get very upset if any of the kids touched the food while he was preparing it. Sometimes he'd get so mad, he'd start talking Gaelic, then chuck all the food away. Off he'd go for a walk to calm down. He'd start all over again when he got back, making something simple like egg and chips, or sausage and chips, to get everyone fed.

Bathing without hot water in the house meant heating water in buckets on the stove, then pouring it in a tin bathtub. Dad washed all the children everyday in that tub, and then used it for doing laundry each Monday, rinsing and wringing everything by hand.

He worked hard, but paid a high price as he got older. Many times, after finishing all the work that had to be done, he had to soak his stiff, swollen hands in ice-water to try and ease the pain in his joints.

My parents were strict, especially about hygiene and manners. They never smacked us, but would tell us off when we got out of line, or use other creative methods of discipline. When I was about five, I cried for hours to my mom for a sixpence. Dad finally put me in a sack and hung it on the back of a door for ten minutes until I calmed down. I did get my sixpence, but worked hard the rest of the day to earn it.

My mom's relatives were frequent visitors to our house, and one of my favorites was her aunt Gensie. She knew just how to make a little boy of four feel special. Whenever Gensie arrived, she'd join my mom on the sofa, both of them ready to watch my show. First I'd stack tin cans in front of them, then grab a couple of sticks and start banging away on my "drums" and singing. I'll always remember the two of them clapping and laughing, encouraging me as I sang and played.

I was about six when my dad died, but Mom told me, "He went away to work."

I'm sure she felt that's all I could cope with at such a young age, but for some unknown reason I had a funny feeling that my dad went to Heaven. When he died, my mom seemed to slow down. She lost interest in life around her, and became bedridden. I'd try to comfort her by laying down beside her, cuddling up and sleeping with her , so she wouldn't feel alone.

Just before my mom's passing, I was amazed to see a brilliant white light in the distance. My dad appeared in that light, drew near to the side of the bed, then just stood there. I pulled the cover over our eyes, Mom's and mine, because I didn't want her to see him. Young as I was, I somehow knew that my mom could still see him, even through the covers.

Two days later, on a damp, rainy Friday evening, my mom passed into the spirit world at forty-nine years old, the same exact age my dad had been when he died. I was in the square across the road with my friends, playing soccer, my favorite sport. When I rushed into the house for something, my brother Danny told me our mother had died, and that I was to go straight to Uncle Tommy's for the night. I was only 13, so I can't remember many details about that night, just the shock and emotional pain.

The family wouldn't let me go to the funeral because I was still too upset, unable to deal with my mother's passing after having already lost my father. I don't even know who was with me on the day of the funeral, or if I stayed at my house or went to one belonging to someone else. But I remember knowing, without a doubt, that Mom was going to "that place" to be reunited with Dad.

I also believe that ever since my mom and dad passed, they've watched over me, and have continued to help me from the spirit world.

My parents' love and support gave me a great foundation, but they couldn't help me in school. I was excited to start at The Fleecefield Infant and Junior School when I turned five, but I struggled with the work from the first day. I can't explain why I tried so hard, but still couldn't do my reading and writing, nor could I learn how to read a clock. It wasn't a lack of love from my parents, nor from my brothers and sisters after our parents died. None of the other children in the family were affected, and I've always wondered what caused my problem.

My difficulties in school continued through secondary school and the first three stages of senior school as well. When there were tests, the teacher would hand me an exam paper right along with the other students, but I didn't know what to do. I'd sit there and scribble on the paper while the other students completed the exam questions. The teachers just pushed me forward to the next class, in spite of my inability to do the work.

During my last year at school, I met a friend named Paul. Every day he would bring in a newspaper with articles about football, or soccer, as they call it in the U.S. I enjoyed looking at the pictures, but Paul showed me how to read the words. When I left school in the fourth year, at age 16, I was recognizing words in the newspaper for the first time.

My older brothers and sisters deserve a medal for holding the family together after our parents died. Michael, the oldest, was an adult when our mother passed away, so he took on the responsibility for the rest of us.

At first, we all remained in the council house, but there were no other grown-ups with us, since Jock had left shortly after dad died. My sisters and brothers had to build their own lives, and began moving into their own places. When I left school at sixteen,

they welcomed me as I drifted back and forth
between their houses.

Coming of Age

My friendship with Paul deepened when we left school, and expanded to include his family. His Mom and Dad, Joyce and Harry, welcomed me into their family as if I were another son. For a few years, as I found my way after leaving school, they were like the Mom and Dad I didn't have.

It was hard trying to find a good job for myself right after school, since reading and writing were special problems for me. I started doing a variety of little jobs, trying to see what I could actually do. I found I liked baking bread and scones, and all those lovely tasty things like donuts and buns.

Perhaps my fondness for bakeries came from living across the road from one. My sisters and lots of other girls called themselves The Hot Wall Gang, standing up against that hot bakery wall, especially on a cold winter's night. I remember being around that wall and waiting for the fresh bread and rolls and donuts to come out of the oven. That's where the girls began calling me "Little Tommy Blue Eyes," since I was the youngest.

When I was around 16, my friend Brian and I would go roller skating every weekend in North London, or go to Bayswater to ice skate. I think we'd go there just to fall on the ice, have fun, and talk to different people. By that time, I'd been having visions, but never dreamed what the future would hold.

One day, when I was about 18, I went into a bakery located just around the corner from where I had a room, and asked the man, Eddie, if he had any work. He took me in straight away, and showed me all the things to do with bread-making, which was super. I got to make bread pudding and all the different kinds of cakes. I specialized in making bread and rolls, and continued working there for many years. When Eddie sold the business, I kept on with the new owners. In time I had an opportunity to work in a small family bakery doing the work I loved.

School and finding a job I enjoyed were difficult for me, but gifts of the spirit came naturally. My brothers and sisters told me our mom was very psychic. As a Romany Gypsy, she would do fortune telling for family members and friends by reading flowers and tea leaves. When I was a small boy, while my parents were still alive, I had an imaginary friend. I used to talk to the little girl, and felt that she was there to help me in some way. I believe she's still with me to this day, a guardian angel from the spirit world to help me in my work.

The invisible little girl disappeared for a few years when I was about 13. My teen-aged interests focused on playing sports and chasing after girls. Those years were spent learning a bit about life and how to handle the responsibilities of working and maintaining my own small flat in Enfield, where I'd moved from Edmonton.

I started having epileptic seizures when I was 20 or so. I didn't know what was happening to me, but was determined not to let the seizures stop me. I was lucky enough to have the love and support of my family and friends, including Paul and his parents. I tried to enjoy myself to the best of my ability during the period when I was having those fits. I went out dancing and to the movies with my friends, and still kept up with sports.

It wasn't until I was in my early twenties that visions started coming to me. I remember lying on my bed one night after I'd turned the light off, when a pure white light came into the room. That light was amazing, something special, like a spiritual sign.

Other things continued to happen while I lived in that flat, like balls of white light moving around the room, and colored moving pictures appearing on the wall, just like on a telly, with people in them. I was even starting to see colorful auras around people. I knew all those things were signs pointing toward my life's future.

My mom's sister, Mary Polten, was a spiritual medium and healer who went around the country to the Spiritualist Churches. She did private readings and healings in her house, located in Bush Hill Park, just over a mile from where I lived.

One day, when I was about 29, Aunt Mary called and invited me to come early for a meeting at her house. Nine of us gathered for a development circle, an event for people who wanted to develop their gifts in healing and mediumship, and to get inspiration for giving talks. Aunt Mary described all those activities before the others arrived, so I'd have an idea of what to expect. She instructed me to sit and relax for the evening. There were some lovely characters there, many of whom came every Tuesday night for spiritual enlightenment. Each person was getting psychic messages from people in the spirit world.

Then my aunt turned to me and said, "Stand up Thomas."

I stood, wondering what she wanted me to do.

She said, "It's your turn, now, to see what you get."

I didn't know what I was going to say, or exactly what I was supposed to do. To my amazement, I found myself giving messages from the spirit world. In fact, I gave a reading to every single person in the circle from dearly loved spirits on the other side. Those spirits brought personal messages and detailed information. Their messages were filled with love, a clear demonstration that the connection to their loved ones hadn't changed when they'd passed on.

Afterwards, my aunt thanked me for coming, and many of the guests asked me if I'd done this before.

"Well," I said, "as a child I had a special spirit friend who'd talk with me. Whenever a spirit is nearby, I can always feel it, especially my mom and dad who are often with me."

Everyone asked if I would come again, but I was overwhelmed that all those people cared about helping me. I wasn't able to tell them if I'd be coming again for sure, because I didn't know if Aunt Mary would ask me back.

To my surprise, after the evening was over, my aunt said, "Now get on with it. You need to do what you were meant to do, work for the spirit world. You've got angels and helpers and spirit guides all around, just waiting for you to start."

Mary went on to tell me that I had a North American Indian guide who works with me and guides me through my life, and that my parents would be there to guide me as well.

I left my aunt's house feeling overwhelmed, and shed many tears that night, confused by the knowledge of what I should be doing. Now, I understand, and describe this path as my calling to help people in need. I believe that my mom and dad, whom I loved so much as a child, are providing me with the strength and guidance I missed because of their early passing.

My aunt's words had given me a lot to think over. About three weeks later, one of the people I'd met at the development circle came into the bakery and told me about a psychic center in a school in Edmonton. He asked me if I'd like to go there and work. Since I'd been born and raised in Edmonton, I agreed to give it a try and see what happened.

To my amazement, I ended up working there for three years. I'd sit at a table with people who needed assistance, and would receive psychic and spiritual messages for them. The staff at that center, who I loved dearly, helped strengthen me through their encouragement and spiritual support, which in turn helped my guides and helpers from the spirit world.

I remember one day, just after I started at the center, having a man named Tom Downing at my table. I believe he's in the spirit world now, but he must have been in his seventies when I gave him a reading.

After receiving his message, Tom told me, "I see you doing spiritual readings and healing in the future."

I understood his words to mean that a door had opened at Aunt Mary's house, and as a result, something very special and powerful was happening.

From the day I started doing this work, when I was 29 until now, I believed the two worlds, the one on this earth plane and the one in the spirit world, were linked together as one. I believe that people who have been seeking contact with the spirits for many years can look at all the experiences of my life, and know, without a doubt, that there is life after death.

The love I received from my parents didn't end when they died. Instead, both Mom and Dad appeared to me from the spirit world when I was a little child, then continued coming to me as I grew up, and have remained with me to this day. All that I learned from my parents, from my brothers and sisters, and other family members, as well as the spirit people I've seen, have helped me understand that the work I do is done with truth and love, and to help people accept that life continues after what we call death.

At the Front of the Church

I was relaxing at home one Sunday afternoon, when I decided to visit a Spiritualist Church I knew was in the area. I'd been working at the Spiritualist Center for awhile, so visiting the church seemed like a good idea. I set out for a walk, asking people for directions. When I reached the main road, I found a sign reading Edmonton Spiritualist Church, Linnell Road. I saw a lovely, bright white light surrounding the words on the sign. I followed the road, and sat down in the back of the room as the church service began.

The individual doing the Sunday service was a gentleman named Anthony Trevor. I was astonished by the accuracy and love that came through in his messages for people in the congregation, and their acceptance of the spirits coming through for them. I felt so much comfort and freedom in the church, in fact, that everything about it radiated peace and harmony.

The welcoming atmosphere felt wonderful, so I began attending on a regular basis.

One Monday, I went to an afternoon service. By this time I was feeling a little braver, so sat closer to the front. Before the services started, people talked among themselves about different events that were coming up, such as a psychic supper. I found it easy to mix with those people, since we were like-minded, and had similar interests.

As we sat there, the committee members were getting a little anxious because the medium scheduled to speak that evening hadn't arrived. Finally they called out asking if there were any psychics among us.

Without thinking, I put my hand up and announced that I was a medium and psychic, and asked if they'd like me to do the service. My mind was on the advice I'd received from my auntie, as she'd guided me and introduced me to the joy of using my gifts to help others.

So, the Church President, Joyce, introduced me by saying, "Our scheduled medium hasn't arrived, but we have a stand-in medium tonight, Mr. Tom Flynn."

When I stood, she asked me to start with a prayer, but to be honest, I was lost. Though I believed in prayer, I was a very ordinary, private person and didn't feel comfortable saying a prayer in front of the church members.

"I'm sorry, can I just get on with the messages?" I asked.

She said, "Certainly, young man." and I found myself standing up on a platform in the front of the room.

To my amazement, I began giving messages of love from the spirit world for many of the people sitting there in front of me. Each spirit brought a special, personal message from beyond for someone they loved.

Being able to pass on those messages gave me a tremendous spiritual lift, and also hope that I'd be able to continue doing good work for the movement and church. When I finished that service, I became a member of the church and continued to attend services. I didn't know what was going to happen in the future, but I was confident that experiences in the church, as well as my work at the Psychic Center, would help me on my path as a medium.

One day, I got a phone call from a lady named Kitty, asking me to do a service at The Beacon of Light Church in Enfield. It would be the first service I did after the one at Edmonton.

Once I'd accepted, I started practicing my prayers so I'd be ready. I'd gotten comfortable speaking to the congregation at the Edmonton Spiritualist Church, but when it came time to do the service at The Beacon of Light, I was shaking in my boots, too nervous to go inside.

I felt tears pooling in my eyes, and found myself asking my mom and dad why I was doing this. Their response was immediate, letting me know that I was to serve as a bridge, or link, between the living and the spirit world. All that I'd experienced as a child, all the love they'd given me, both before and after their passing, was to provide inspiration so I could become an instrument for the work between the two worlds.

I took a deep breath, and walked inside. I was ready to say a prayer, but the speaker asked me to stand up and give a talk on Spiritualism first. I opened my heart and started talking about my personal story, and my purpose in life. I told them about the intense pain of losing my parents as a child, and then losing one of my brothers when he was in his early thirties.

He'd apparently left a cigarette burning on the side of his bed and inhaled the smoke. He was in a coma for a while, before the machines were disconnected.

Losing those three was emotional agony, but then they reached out to me from the spirit world, letting me know they were still here, and still loved me. They taught me how important it is to help the people in spirit keep giving their love and guidance back to the living.

When it came time for the clairvoyance part of giving messages, I found myself directed to a lady and man sitting in the back of the room. As I focused on them I had a vision of a lady and a child, water and a ship. I saw the child slip from the mother's arm, and they both went to the spirit world. The husband survived to tell the tale. I spoke to the couple after the service, and they told me I'd seen what was called the Zeebrugge Disaster, where they'd lost a daughter and a grandchild.

Before I left church that day, a famous medium named Marie Taylor came up to me to compliment me on a lovely service, and to wish me luck. She said my spirit guides wanted me to keep up the work, but that I also needed to play the part. Look the part, was what she meant by that, as she told me to wear a jacket and tie and always go with my feelings.

Walking home that evening, I was lost in childhood memories, and remembered my favorite possession as a little boy was a blanket of Scottish plaid. Mom had a great connection with Scotland, where she had some relatives. From the moment she gave me the plaid blanket, I wouldn't let it go. The only way she could wash it was to take it when I was asleep, and even then I'd hold it tight in my hands.

The blanket is long gone, but now I hold tight to my new life with the same passion.

Spreading His Wings

On a rainy Wednesday evening right after the 1985 New Year, I headed to a Spiritualist Church in Eltham, London. I'd received an invitation to serve the church from a woman who lived on the outskirts of London. I'd just started doing my mediumship work in churches, and once again was welcomed with warmth, kindness, and open hearts. I enjoyed every minute as I stood on the platform that evening, sharing messages coming through from the spirit world.

Throughout that year, many other churches in London and surrounding areas continued to contact me to serve them. I loved the work, but sometimes wondered how to get more confidence, experience, and knowledge to do an even better job.

Right on time, in answer to my prayers, a lovely couple, Sue and Dave, invited me to their house where they were running a development circle, where a small people come together to learn more about their spiritual gifts. They were great personalities, both giving their time to the people working to develop their spiritual gifts, and serving in the Cat Protection League, helping to find homes for cats in need.

Our group of seven were all in tune with each other, and we supported one other in the development of our different gifts. Some were spiritual healers, others were gifted speakers with the ability to inspire people, and others were mediums. Over a period of 18 months, we worked and grew together.

One of the most wonderful experiences was when my sister, Phyllis, who's a natural psychic, joined us for a special event. We put up a Christmas tree and invited all the spirit children to come and celebrate with us.

I opened with a prayer, we sang Christmas songs, then we all did a short meditation and linked into the spirit world to see what messages we could get. There was a short period of silence afterwards, then we shared the messages we'd received, some of which were about Christmas memories.

As we sat there in silence, we heard a rapping sound coming from the Christmas tree, and then the soft sound of bells ringing on the tree. Some of the people in the circle experienced feelings of coldness around them, a sign that spirits were drawing close to them.

Others felt soft touches on their shoulders, their back, and their hair. Phyllis told us there were children from the spirit world in that room with us. I was also seeing children from the spirit world who belonged to people in the circle.

For the children, Christmas night turned out to be wonderful, and one of my fondest memories.

As I continued working as a medium, I started getting write-ups in the Psychic News. Just a few years into my mediumship, a gentleman called for an appointment because of a recommendation by the Psychic News. He was a visitor to London from the United States. I can't remember our exact conversation, but do know he walked out with a smile on his face, having received comfort from his family.

He thanked me for the messages he'd received, and said, "You never know, you may be making a visit to the United States one day."

I told him to remember that his loved ones were close, and that he could talk to them just like he did when they were alive. Sending a thought pattern to them, which doesn't have to be out loud, can reach them can be as easy as having lovely thoughts and meaningful prayers.

For two nights running, five years into my spiritual development, I saw little old ladies in scarves during my dreams. I also saw a clear white light and some children. Right away I started pulling the children out of the darkness into the light. Three or four weeks later, I found myself proving survival after death to several people who had lost children.

One of them was a lady who had waited seven years for survival evidence, after traveling all over the country from London to Scotland. She told me all she wanted was a particular person from the spirit world to come forward.

I said, "Don't give me any information. All I want is to hear your voice, my voice, and Spirit's voice." I reached out to the spirit world, and a little girl of about three came forward. She took me to the brick wall in the garden and told me that the wall had fallen on top of her. The little girl said, "Mommy tried to lift the wall off me, and it left a scar on mommy's left knee."

The lady then showed me her left knee with a scar in exactly the spot the little girl had pointed to. The woman didn't want to know anything else. She went home happy.

The Psychic News published a story about that little girl and her mom, which brought a call from another lady in Liverpool. As we talked, messages started coming through. The woman who called also had a little girl in the spirit world who moved close to me as we talked. She was thrilled, since it was the first contact she'd had with her daughter, even though she'd been to many mediums.

One day, a couple came in with a small white coffin. I really didn't know what to say to them, so I just talked with them, prayed, and gave love and guidance from the spirit world. Then they walked out. I was overwhelmed by the situation, but knew Spirit was telling me to guide them and tell them that the child was all right.

Having the value of my work recognized in print was wonderful. The publicity generated wider interest and brought a call from a woman named Sandie, inviting me to come to Jersey in the Channel Islands. Sandie arranged several meetings with people she knew, so I could assist them through spiritual healing and messages. As always, I'd start each session with a prayer and an affirmation of my firm belief that life continues when we leave this world.

That 1987 trip was my very out of the country, just a few years into my mediumship.

I continued working through churches in London after returning from Jersey, and began branching out to Spiritualist Churches in Hertfordshire and other small counties outside of London.

Some people who came for readings were unsure about what to expect from me. They were seeking comfort, reaching out in the hope of some contact from someone they'd lost, but didn't know what to do.

My advice was always the same. If you go to a healer or medium, just have an open mind, and trust your feelings. Life does continue after this world, and the spirit world is there for us if we remember to have an open mind.

In the early 1990s, a man named George called me, asking for some spiritual communication on the phone. I asked him what sort of reading he wanted, from the past, present or for guidance? He said he wanted to communicate with the spirit world, and wanted to tape the reading.

When a medium reads on the phone, all the caller get is voices, my voice, the person I'm talking with, and the spirits. I first gave George the colors green for relaxing and healing, because he was nervous. As I was linking, a lady came through, saying she was his wife. I described his wife's appearance and her character, and then passed on her messages about little things they'd done, and memories they shared.

George was over the moon with all the details his wife gave him, and of the knowledge of her continuous existence since leaving the world. He felt wonderful knowing he could communicate with his wife, and that she was listening to the prayers he was sending to her. She was aware of the flowers that he used to put out for her. He knew from the messages that his wife was still very much with him, and it gave him so much joy, laughter, and tears all at the same time.

After that reading, George often phoned me to tell me he listens to the recording over and over again. He said each time he listened was like receiving healing, for his body, his mind, and his spirit.

My greatest joy was the experience of helping all the people who came my way, with the spirit world using me as that channel for them.

Mediums & Healers

For about six years, I worked with another medium, Tony Katz, in the London area. Tony was a psychic artist, in addition to being a medium. When we were together, I'd stand up and start the service with prayers, while Tony'd sit still and wait for his communication with the spirit world. His guides helped him do his psychic work, just as mine would provide information and love from the spirit world to members of the congregation.

One time, when we were in Hertfordshire, I was instructed to send healing to people in need who were feeling lonely, in pain or just stressed. So, I asked the members of the audience if anyone was having a problem with their lower back.

A lady put her hand up and said, "Yes, it's me."

I told her I'd send some healing to her through my spirit guide, and that we'd come back to her in a little while. I continued on with my messages for

about ten minutes, then turned back to
the lady and asked her how she felt. She
told me she felt relaxed and free of
pain. We both thanked the spirit and
guides for their help.

I was curious about who was
working with me from the spirit world,
and discovered that Tony Katz had
drawn a picture of my guide. He said
the guide's name was Dr. Joseph
Eisenberg.

As I visited other Spiritualist
Churches, quite often someone would
come up to me saying, "There is a man
here who has white hair and beard who
would like to work with you from the
spirit world." Their descriptions were
always a match with Tony's picture of
my healing guide.

A gentleman named Aidan Clark
spoke to me when I was speaking at a
Spiritualist Church in Stockwell,
London, and said. "I have a gentleman
here I believe is your spirit guide."
Aidan Clark not only described who he
said was my spiritual healer, but handed
me a picture he'd drawn that looked just
like the image created by Tony.

The same exact thing happened at a
third church, where I received another
picture of my spiritual healing guide. I
now had three pictures, all of the same

person, proof to me that the healing door had been opened. All I'd done was keep my heart open and the gift of healing was given.

Tom with the picture of Dr. Joseph Eisenberg drawn by Tony Katz

I call myself a natural medium and healer, but if someone had told me years ago that I'd be doing spiritual readings and healing, I probably would have laughed. The spirit world has helped me from the time I was a child. When I was about seven or eight, I was playing in Pyms Park in Edmonton, running, chasing and playing with a ball, when I fell in the lake. My sister jumped in and saved me. It was quite traumatic, since I was terrified of drowning.

Another time, just after my dad died, my sister Phyllis and I were playing outside, when a man came toward us and asked if we'd like him to take us to a store and buy some sweets. Phyllis was going to go with him, but a voice in my head told me not to let her go.

"My dad's over there." I said, as I grabbed her hand and ran away with her.

Both of those incidents make me thankful to my parents for teaching us the right and wrong of things. I believe the spirit world protected my sisters and me because God had plans for our future.

Messages from the spirit world aren't restricted to formal readings. While I was working in the bakery, a lady came up to me and asked what her baby would be.

I said, "Well, I guess you'll have twins."

"Twins," she said, in total disbelief.

"Yes, you'll have twin boys."

About six weeks later, she came back into the bakery to tell me the doctor had confirmed she was carrying twin boys. She was thrilled because she wanted to have boys.

My sister Phyllis called one day because of problems at home. Her fridge and washing machine weren't working right, and she had cold spots in the passageway and in the bedroom.

She asked me to come around and try to figure out what to do. I said a prayer, then reached out to the spirit. I knew the spirit was someone who'd lived in the house before. The spirit remained on the property because it helped people feel close to those they'd loved. I reached out and discovered the spirit was a lady who'd loved her family and the house where they'd lived.

"You're not wanted in this dwelling." I told her. "Just reach out to the light and go to the spirit world."

Phyllis and I, to our amazement, stood there and heard a WHHHOOOSSSHHH sound, and saw a white mist. When the mist cleared, we went downstairs and had a cup of tea. We waited for about half an hour, and then went back upstairs. The hallway and the bedroom area were at peace, and were warm where they had never been warm before. Phyllis felt the peace and the love return. Helping that spirit person go to the light was fantastic.

Stonehenge

Another door opened for me spiritually when a young Spanish couple called me to their home in a London area. Their little boy kept saying someone was coming close to him. I linked in and began describing a man.

The husband said, "It's impossible."

I asked, "What's impossible?"

And he answered, "You're describing my brother. He died in Spain."

I told the husband earth locations don't matter. If he called upon the spirit world, they'd respond, no matter where he happened to be. That little boy was a lovely lad, and the spirit was a lovely, pure lad too. They were like two brilliant, shining lights that had connected.

The father was pleased his brother's spirit had returned, and communicated with his son. He and his wife were happy and thankful to learn that there're no time or distance limitations in the spirit world, and that spirits can travel in an instant to share messages and love.

Another of my home experiences was with a lady who called about problems the family was having with their daughter. Once again, I went to the house and described the person who was visiting the little girl. It turned out to be the lady's mother, who wanted to be close to the grandchild.

That was a great experience for them -- to know the mother was close to them. The little girl was seeing her grandmother, and now the family understood and accepted what was happening.

That family reminded me of when I was visited by my own imaginary friend as a child. Now I know she was a girl from the spirit world, whom I believe is still helping me, working as my spirit guide.

I understood that my duties in life were to help people, so I continued working in the London and surrounding areas, both in private homes and in churches. The church services involved spiritual mediumship and healing, while work in private homes also involved clairvoyance and communicating with the spirit people dwelling in the houses. The most important thing for me was remaining open and ready for whenever and however I was needed.

One day, I received a telephone call asking if I'd like to go to Stonehenge and sit around the stones. It was an exciting invitation, and I soon found myself on a train, headed for an adventure with people I'd never met.

This group was composed of myself, many other psychics and mediums, as well as one man in dress as a North American Indian. Although we didn't know one another, we were like-minded, reaching out to the spirit world, asking for assistance from the spirit guides to help people. We all sat down around the stones, and remained there for about half the day, meditating.

For the first time, I discovered I could go into a slight trance and feel the strength and love of the spirits who were there with us. I can't remember the words that came out of my mouth, but the people with me understood. What a fascinating experience. Since then, I've chosen not to trance. I'm more comfortable helping people face to face, remaining in control and using my own voice.

I found myself attending different church services all across England, like the Stockwell Spiritualist Church. Listening and learning from others helped me by providing guidance for my spiritual journey. We should never stop learning. Helping others can be an important part of our own progression. I had a small development circle, about seven people, who met in my Enfield flat every Monday night. I learned that the progress I made for myself depended on what I put into helping others in the circle.

Helping others headed in a new direction when I started doing charity work. I met a lady whose daughter had major health problems. They'd traveled to different hospitals, and at each one had been told she needed an operation. The family couldn't afford to go to Budapest, which they'd been advised to do. I offered to try a healing, and asked Tony Katz to do a psychic reading for her. Thanks to the spirits, the evening with the family and their little girl turned out to be a successful.

Some time later, I was part of a demonstration with five other mediums just outside London. There, I met a lady named Linda, who not only believed in healing, but also worked for the Irish RSPCA, the Irish Society for the Prevention of Cruelty to Animals. She contacted the RSPCA, and set up an evening of clairvoyance for the animal kingdom. The event was a big success, and all the proceeds went to the charity.

Thinking of charity reminds me of an incident that took place two years before I left school. I used to receive school dinners for free because both my parents had died. When I got home each day, my brothers and sisters would feed me things like eggs, sausage, and beans, so we survived.

One day, the schoolteacher said, "May I take you to a shop."

I was surprised, but said, "Yes."

He bought me a pair of trousers and shoes. When I came back shining with "me new trousers and me new shoes on," some of the people didn't recognize me. I don't remember the teacher's name, but I'll always remember his kindness.

When my mom was still alive, I worked at a market on the green in Lower Edmonton. The owner, Freddie, always gave me a big basket of bananas and other food to take home to my mom to help us kids get through the week. His generosity was life saving for us.

London to Chesterfield

Telephone readings were a wonderful way to help people from different areas. One of my first was a lady named Sylvia, from Derbyshire. When giving a reading, I always tell people to have an open mind, say only yes or no, and hopefully the person they're looking for will come through. I also give the color of their aura during the reading. Sylvia's color was mauve, which represented the strength to go forward, and the ability to be uplifted in spirit. As I connected to Sylvia, her husband came through. He described her to me, and told me about her character. He also told about the long life they'd shared, and about his departure to the spirit world. It's marvelous to be able to do that for people.

Another telephone reading was for Lynn, who lived in Bristol. She suffered from agoraphobia, which made it almost impossible for her to leave the house. She phoned me every week for about a year of healing, and sometimes I gave her a reading as well. The last time I spoke to her, she told me she'd gone Christmas shopping for the first time. I was thrilled to know what progress could be achieved when the spirit world used me to help someone in need.

When a lady from Derbyshire called and asked me to speak to the Spiritualist Church there, I accepted right away, with no idea how that invitation would change my life. I did an evening of clairvoyance, and then spoke at a Spiritualist Church in Chesterfield, a market town and a borough of Derbyshire.

I felt so drawn to Derbyshire, that after six months of going there to do my work, I decided to move there. I never, ever would have imagined I'd leave my home in Enfield, and get corporation housing in Chesterfield.

My sisters were very concerned about my decision to live so far away, and kept asking me how I would live, and how did I know I was doing the right thing.

I understood their concern, but knew I had to go for some reason. My good friend, Paul, who'd helped me with reading and writing in my last year of school, helped me load up a van to take all my things to Derbyshire. My friend Brian helped too. They thought I was crazy moving 150 miles away from London and all my early surroundings, and away from all of my family, and friends; however, I knew I was doing the right thing.

New doors opened for me in Derbyshire, and new things started to happen. At one of my demonstrations, I met a man named Reginald Munks, who we called Reg. He said we had a lot in common, such as a love of music and Elvis Presley.

During a past life regression, we discovered a shared memory from our past lives. I told Reg that in my most recent past life I was French. I had seen myself in the engine room of a ship, stoking the fire, when disaster struck. I was on fire, and had to jump overboard to save myself. Reg had the same experience, but he'd been up on deck and damaged his shoulder. He still has that damaged shoulder from his past life.

The effects of that past life on me were different. As a little child I fell in the water and nearly drowned, and have always been afraid of fire. Most little boys love the fire brigade, but I'd always run from the firemen like a scared rabbit. I know lots of people get seasick, but I get sick every single time I'm on the water.

I enjoyed my three years in Derbyshire, learning and growing a lot. From my home there, I traveled to Spiritualist Churches in Yorkshire, Lancastershire, Newcastle, and Glasgow in Scotland. I also continued doing charity work, spiritual healing, readings, services, and spreading love and kindness wherever possible.

I met some very interesting mediums and healers in Derbyshire. One lady, Joan Ormsworth, invited me round to her house once a week for a gathering of people with different ailments.

Joan's face always lit up with a warm smile when I'd arrive. "Would you like a nice cup of tea, Tom, before you start the healing?"

She was such a kind and considerate lady, and now she's gone through the door. I know she still spreads happiness to people in the spirit world, and welcomes those arriving from the earth plane.

One gentleman came to the gathering at Joan's house after he'd suffered a stroke. He couldn't hold a spoon to eat, and was a little off balance. He had faith that he'd get some help, and continued coming to me. To his amazement, he received great help from my guides in the spirit world.

Another lady in England used to send me poems every couple of weeks. Her poems had different meanings, but all shared a common theme about reaching out to people and to God, on the highest. A lot of the poems had to do with angels from spirit. I'm still thankful for all the poems she sent to me.

In 1997, a lady named Jessie was the first person to invite me to Yorkshire. She brought a few people to her house for me to talk to. Jessie had been a great friend of a famous Irish-Canadian medium, who'd passed into the spirit world. She had many friends in Canada, and asked if I'd like to go there to work. When I said yes, she contacted people in Vancouver and Calgary, and they invited me over.

When I went to Canada for the first time, the people were welcoming, and took good care of me. And the scenery in Calgary! I'd walk down the road and I could look right up at the Rocky Mountains. They were absolutely magnificent.

My greatest success in the Spiritualist Churches in Vancouver was with a lad of three. He'd suffered a stroke, and his parents asked if I could do a healing. I asked my spirit guides to send healing energy. I felt my dad working among them. The little boy had a useless arm and hand, but the spirit world worked wonders during the three times I saw him.

A lady named Joan Gordon came and watched me several times in the Spiritualist Churches in Vancouver. After the events, we'd talk and share memories. She told me about coping with the loss of her husband, and was so pleased when her husband came through with messages for her.

Joan was big into charity work, and seemed to take a great interest in me. She wanted to show me different places, and suggested Los Angeles in America. She had friends there who might help me and get me work. Joan said I needed someone to put me up or guide me in the right direction. What I needed was a real connection to take me to America.

When I returned to Derbyshire after my first trip to Canada, I sent distant healing each day to a lady I'd met there named Eileen. The doctors in the hospital had told her and her family that there was nothing more they could do, but it could be days, weeks, or months before she died. The distant healing from me, as well as the prayers and healing she received from others in Calgary, gave her the strength and love she needed to stay a little longer for the people she loved.

I returned for a second time within a year to see Eileen, and give her a contact healing.

I also served two Spiritualist Churches there. It was wonderful to visit all the people I knew in Canada, and to do a little sightseeing. I visited an Indian camp, and watched the Vancouver Ducks play soccer, thanks to a wonderful couple, Tom and Annie, who looked after me in West Vancouver. The people I met made me feel so relaxed, and so much at home. They accepted me for what I was, and welcomed me with open arms.

I also worked on some of the effects of my past life regression while I was in Canada. I was staying in Alberta with a couple and their family. The husband was a fire chief, and he took me into the small fire station where he worked. He took several pictures of me trying on the fireman's outfit.

When the pictures were developed, there was a brilliant beam of light shining right through me, even though there hadn't been any visible light source in the room. We knew it had to do with the spirit world being very close to me.

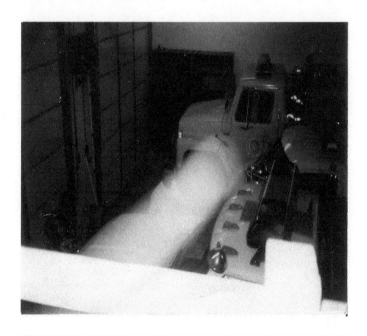

Picture showing hidden light in dark room

Walking among the mountains of Vancouver Island brought me spiritual growth, strength, and energy, even though they felt like they were right on top of me. I felt such peace there, and not just for myself. I knew my mom and dad were with me, driving me forward as a medium and healer, and providing encouragement for me to continue to travel to different places.

New Horizons, Old Memories

Back in Derbyshire, I continued to meet new friends. Reg, who was also a healer and now a Reiki Master, was one of them, together with his wife Linda, also a Reiki Master.

I met my next new friend, Vivienne Brocklehurst, at the Chesterfield Psychic Study Group. Vivienne ran the center where the group met, and gave different speeches every week. She didn't just talk about mediumship, but all kinds of spiritual topics, including healing, past lives, and UFO's.

Those meetings made for wonderful Tuesday nights out. Vivienne encouraged me to keep going forward and to keep helping people as a medium.

London was a great city with lots going on, but it wasn't until I moved to Derbyshire that doors started to open for me. I met a trance medium from Spain named Raymond Smith when he visited Chesterfield. He invited me to his healing sanctuary and psychic center for a week, and had me doing demonstrations and healing while I was there.

As my work expanded, I started getting calls from other mediums, just to encourage me on my spiritual path.

Steven O'Brien, a famous medium, phoned me and said, "Keep the good work of Spiritualism in your heart, and continue with your journey of working for the spirit world."

The encouragement and support from people working in Spiritualism was wonderful, but my family also stayed close. They kept in contact and called often, knowing how important they were to me. Sometimes I'm surprised at all the love and support I receive. I consider myself a very ordinary, down-to-earth, determined person, who understands how to reach out, make things work, and knows how important it is to ask for guidance.

I was invited to come to Belgium by a family whose 22-year-old daughter had trouble walking, and this time Reg went with me. We crossed the sea by ship, and I was on my back from seasickness again. The sea was so rough, everything was falling off the shelves. Good thing Reg was with me, since I passed out once and he had to bring me round.

Reg held the daughter's hands during the session. I placed my hands on her knees and reached out to spirit, asking my guide, Dr. Eisenberg, to come forward. The half hour session with the girl, we reached out to the highest spirits available.

A short time after the healing, we got a call on our mobile phone telling us to look out the window. We saw the young lady walking near the sea with no support, no crutches or cane. Reg kept in contact with the family, and later went back to visit them. Each time he talked to the family on the phone, I'd say a few words as well.

* * *

When I was a teenager I loved soccer, and played with friends on a team called Kingfisher. I went dancing on weekends, and played snooker on Wednesdays. Pretty normal, but I didn't pass my driving test until I was in my thirties. Soon afterwards, I bought my very first car, a little white Fiat. I got it from a friend who owned a car repair garage. We'd met when I gave him a reading where his son came through. It touched him deeply, and we became friends. We'd often go to Spiritualist Churches together to watch other mediums.

I loved that little car, and drove it to a weekend booking at a Spiritualist Church in Wales. I'd been to Wales before, but that was the first time I'd driven by myself. After doing the service, I stayed overnight and drove back the next morning. On the way back, I heard a police siren. They pulled me over and said, "Have you been drinking?"

I said, "That's right."

"How many did you have?"

I answered, "Two."

They told me they were going to have to take me into the station, but first I'd have to take a breathalyzer test. One kept asking how many drinks I'd had, saying he could smell alcohol on my breath. I took the breathalyzer, but the reading was normal.

I said to the officer, "I had two cups of tea."

I didn't know if he'd laugh or "turn me face." It was pretty funny for my first trip in the car.

A local man, with a slipped disc in his back, was coming to my flat for spiritual healing. I laid my hands on him for twenty minutes, after which he stood up, feeling at peace and free of pain.

I told him, "You should thank my spirit guides, and also the greatest spirit of them all, the holy spirit."

He remained with me for about an hour, talking about all the different experiences he'd had in life. He asked me how I'd become a healer and medium. We talked, drank tea, and laughed and joked some more, then he thanked me again for the healing.

I said, "Don't thank me, thank the spirit guide who used me for the spirit of love."

Then he asked me how long I'd been in Derbyshire, and how long I intended to stay.

I said, "At the moment I want to stay here always. I really feel comfortable and relaxed in Derbyshire, and the people I've met have been very nice, kind, and considerate."

Moving to a small town in Derbyshire from London had been a huge step, and resulted in my experiencing a different way of life. I felt my friends and loved ones in the spirit had guided me toward the move to provide me with more peace of mind, and to help me grow stronger as a medium.

Because I love all kinds of music, I'd often spent Sunday evenings at a pub around the corner from where I lived. I'd sit there, enjoying the singers each night. The music would take me back to my childhood when my sister Felicia and I would sit outside a local bar on the weekends, with our Pepsi Cola or orange juice, while our mom was inside with her brother and friends.

The bar had an old piano, and Mom would sing along all the good, old-time songs. She really enjoyed going with her brother, Tommy, for a chance to get away from being stuck at home.

Tommy is in the spirit world with her now, and I'll bet they're having a good laugh remembering those times. Two of my brothers are also in the spirit world with them. Raymond passed from a house fire, and my oldest brother Michael died at fifty-eight from cancer. I know they're all together, guiding my brothers and sisters and me through our lives.

I often dream of my loved ones who've passed on. My mom and dad, and my brothers Raymond and Mickey, which is what we called Michael, all come to me in my dreams. They take me to visit lovely, calm places like countrysides where I can hear birds singing in the trees, or the sound of water flowing, or the smell of the sweet scent of flowers. It's marvelous how refreshing and healing those peaceful dreams are to the soul.

Thinking of family, reminds me of one special Christmas. Mom always used to decorate the tree on Christmas Eve. There were special bells on the tree, and a little pink one for the top, put in place by one of the older boys. We'd all stay up late on Christmas Eve, but my sister Phyllis and I were always the last to go to bed because we were waiting for Father Christmas.

There were times when we stayed awake until six o'clock in the morning, waiting for Christmas to come. When we all woke up a couple of hours later, there would be one little present for each of us, which we were grateful for.

Reg and I continued with the Tuesday night meetings at the Spiritualist Church, where I would stand in when the medium didn't turn up. I'd share the platform with a psychic lady named Angie, who also played the piano for the music part of the service.

She's now passed into the spirit world, but back then, Reg and I spent many hours at her house enjoying cups of tea, conversation, and meditation, plus lots of talking and planning.

One day I asked Vivienne if I could do a flower sense evening, like my mom had done. About forty people turned up that night, each with a flower, which they put in a vase before taking their seats. Each vase was a colorful bouquet of varied blossoms, including many of my mom's favorites. Then all the vases were brought forward and placed on a table near me.

Holding each flower, one by one, I had no idea who'd brought it. Messages came with each flower. Afterwards I'd ask who had brought the flower, and whether the message had meaning for that person.

One of the messages got me in trouble. The message from one flower was that the person was going to attend a musical concert. No one raised a hand, so I asked who'd brought that flower. The gentleman identified himself, but kept insisting that he had no plans to attend a concert, even though my message was strong and very clear.

Finally the man's wife spoke up. "Yes, he's going to a music concert. I bought the tickets already, but the concert was supposed to be a surprise for his birthday. Guess it's not a surprise, now."

I must have stood there for over two hours, reading the flowers for members of the congregation, feeling my mom's presence with me the whole time.

Spain & Australia

From my base in Derbyshire, I worked as a medium in two other lovely counties, Devon and Cornwall. I visited different Spiritualist Churches for special evenings and workshops. By that time, I was more confident, and had the courage to help other people to develop their own gifts.

During a workshop, we'd meditate, talk about the purpose of our lives, and do little projects. Sometimes I'd have them draw a house, a tree, a fence, the sun, and a back yard full of flowers. Then they'd pass the drawing to the person next to them and see what they got from it.

That experience was a little bit of psychology and intuitiveness, and should reveal something about the artist's personality. If someone drew a big house, he was open. If he drew a small house, he was a homebody. A summer tree showed the artist liked life, while a spring tree showed a quieter person less fond of bright sunshine.

We also did a little psychometry, where people would hold an object, such as a ring or watch, and see what information they learned from it.

In addition, I'd teach them the basics of spiritual healing, how to lay hands on the person, touching the head or back. Since some people aren't comfortable with being touched, I'd demonstrate how to place hands near the body, without touching, and still send healing energy.

My next trips were to Spain. My first was to Gibraltar, where I gave a reading to a lady named Sylvia.

The trip after that was in response to an invitation from Terry and Jess, a couple who asked me join them for healing at their sanctuary in Tenerife, on the Canary Islands. Together we did different kinds of healing circles and development exercises, and worked with my spiritual healing guide, Dr. Eisenberg.

In Tenerife I met a fascinating man named John, who seemed to know all about every star and planet in the sky. John and I must have talked for three hours. The information he shared was way over my head, but I could have listened to him all night.

A lady named Sheila invited me to Shakespeare's country, in the English Midlands. I went to her home to do spiritual work many times, and then worked in Spiritualist Churches in the area. From that work came an opportunity to travel to Sydney, Australia, to meet with friends of hers.

During the spring of 1998 after I arrived there, I traveled all over the Sydney area, including the Blue Mountains. The nearby lakes had water so pure one could scoop it up in your hand and drink it. The couple who invited me, David and Jane, had set up an all-day healing workshop at a Spiritualist Church near the Blue Mountains.

During the workshop I talked about my path into Spiritualism, and how I was guided to work in spirit with my guardian angels, loved ones, and spirit guides.

We talked about the chakras -- the crown chakra, the third eye chakra, the throat chakra, the heart chakra, the solar plexus chakra, and the base chakra-- as well as the colors and energies connected with each.

Then we talked together about spiritual healing. The people who attended that day shared their personal experiences.

One member who joined in our circle was an American tourist who was suffering tremendous pain from a hairline fracture to his shoulder. I explained that all I could do was to reach out to my guides and helpers, and let them use me as a symbol of love, and then see what happens. Everybody tuned in as one and focused on helping him take in the energy of spiritual healing. After the healing, he stood up, free of pain.

I was told one particular church in the Blue Mountains usually had about ten people attend their Sunday services, but when I did an evening of clairvoyance, about 150 people came. I did a service with flowers, but it was a little different because in Australia they use the centers of the flowers to bring in the spirit.

Miss Sheila took me everywhere I needed or wanted to go in Australia, including three Spiritualist Churches. One of the greatest moments was at a church just outside of Newcastle. I shared the platform with an Aboriginal lady in full costume. I stood, on the platform giving out messages, but mediums differ in the way they work, and this lady went into the congregation to give messages.

Afterward we shared moments of the service with each other and with her husband. He was a great person, with deep knowledge of the spirit.

Sheila and I had a great day sightseeing. We got to visit an animal sanctuary, where me met koalas, ostriches, and kangaroos. She also took me to see the very first bank of Australia. It was just a little hut with the sign, "The Bank of Australia."

Malaysia, Pain & Blessings

When I returned from Australia, I continued on my spiritual path, but I also continued to enjoy things on a personal level. Reg and I went to clubs and sang karaoke. Reg would start, and then pull me up front with him. He sang Elvis, and I sang Cliff Richard.

One day, I got a telephone call from a woman, who I'll call Lily, in Kuala Lumpur, Malaysia. By this time, The Psychic News was printing articles about me that opened doors to other countries. Lily called because she needed my help.

The flight was 18 hours from England. When I arrived, Lily and her husband welcomed me and took me into their home.

"Today we will let you rest and get over your long journey."

I woke up the next morning feeling fresh and ready to work. Lily asked lots of questions about my spiritual work, and about how long I'd been doing it. By that time I'd been working with the spirit world for fourteen years. She continued with bombarding me with questions, and then wanted to sit in on several of my readings.

I said, "You'll get experience and understand how I work by just watching me do demonstrations or talking about healing and Spiritualism."

Lily wasn't satisfied, and insisted on sitting in on the readings, even wanting to tape them and keep the tapes. I'd sit opposite the person I was reading, while she stayed on my right hand side throughout. Since Lily made all the arrangements and invited everyone who came, the guests and I were in awkward positions.

I told her the readings were private, a one-to-one conversation, but Lily insisted and sat there through readings for ten people. The second day was exactly the same, even though I tried to tell her I was not happy at all with this situation. The people didn't seem to care, which surprised me.

The third day started out the same, but the first woman waiting for a reading pointed to Lily and asked, "Have you been reading this lady?"

I said, "No, she brought me here and wants to sit in."

"But this is private." The woman said. "Do you mind if she doesn't sit in."

I said it would be fine, and Lily stood up and left for the rest of the day.

The tenth and last reading of the day was for a Chinese Malay businessman I'll call Umar, a kind and considerate person. He was comforted by his reading, which was from someone he had loved dearly. For some unknown reason, Umar stayed behind when we were through, and followed me into another room where Lily was waiting.

She said, "Tom, we'll have to put you in a hotel tomorrow."

I thought, put me in a hotel? I couldn't understand that part. I asked her why, and she repeated that I'd have to go to a hotel.

I said, "I believe, in all honesty, that the reason why you want to put me in a hotel is because you couldn't sit in on the readings."

Lily got a little bit angry, and said, "Tom, get out. "She told me to leave her friend's house, and leave hers as well. I asked for my two-day's worth of money, not that it mattered at that point. When I left her house, I'd need some food and some place to stay.

The Chinese Malay man, Umar, was by my side through the ugly scene, and offered to help me. He took me to get my belongings from Lily's house, then to a hotel where I stayed for two days until he got me a return flight home.

My plans had turned upside down. I'd been offered a place in the home of the couple who invited me, and said they'd take care of food, transportation, and everything else I'd need. Instead, I was turned away after three days, 18,000 miles away from home.

Umar was an angel in human form. He told me the reason why he helped me was because when he'd broken his leg, a German man carried him all the way to the hospital. He passed the kindness on to me, and made sure I was taken to a place I'd be welcome. He also took me to his workplace, to his clubhouse, and even asked me to join him for a night out.

In addition to meeting my Malaysian rescuer, one other good thing came out of my trip to Malaysia. I looked at other spiritual aspects of Kuala Lumpur. I had my aura read, and pictures taken so I could see the colors that were around me. I also went to a healer. There were separate rooms for men and women, and the healers were blind men.

I went up to one of the healers and asked him, "Could I receive some healing from your guides and helpers from the spirit?"

I sat down, and he started giving me general healing to relax me. Then, all of a sudden, he turned around and said, "May I give you a massage to the back?"

I said, "Certainly."

He had me lie down on a little bench, and then he was standing on my back, massaging me with his feet, his full weight on top of my back. That was crazy, but so comforting.

I got safely back to Derbyshire and carried on with my spiritual work. Then I received a call from a gentleman in London, asking me to serve their church in Acton.

I said, "Certainly, but I'll have to catch a very early train and spend the day, then get back the very next day."

He replied, "Certainly. We'll pay your fare."

He'd been the booking secretary when I first served that church ten years before, and was very complimentary. He also sent me his short list of ten mediums and told me he'd just added my name to it, and said, "The good people in your neighborhood will have to get their sliced bread elsewhere."

His words uplifted my spirits from the bad experience in Malaysia. Spirit does indeed work in mysterious ways.

While I was serving at the Acton Spiritualist Church, I met with a good friend and fellow psychic, Jeffrey Phillips. I was happy to see him again, since we'd worked together before and got along very well. Going back home on the motorway, I thought about the day, and how it showed me spirit gives encouragement and opens doors when it's meant to be.

Chesterfield to Ireland

Carnfield Hall dates back to the 1470s, and is said to be one of the most haunted properties in Britain. I went there with my friend Reg and a spiritual study group from Chesterfield, in Derbyshire.

The owner showed us around, taking about an hour to go through the different rooms. You could feel the cold spots in the rooms. At one place I saw a lovely white spirit light. I'd say the spirits dwelling in that house have been there for a very long time. They weren't there to haunt the place. They lived there, simple as that.

A friend of mine invited me to a birthday party, and to my surprise, a newspaper article was written about it, titled *Tom Comes to Tea*. Someone, who then arranged a healing session for a man with difficulty seeing, saw the article. I asked my spirit guide, Doctor Eisenberg, to come through to help this gentleman.

After the healing, he was able to see things again, and took great joy in strolling through his garden. I thought that was fantastic. Through the spirit guides and *Tom Comes to Tea*, that gentleman was helped.

I was living a good life, helping people through the spirits, and even having articles written about me. Thinking about those things makes me remember how very different life was when I was growing up.

My mom used to put sticks at the bottom of the fire, and then put on coal we'd bought from the coal men. But sometimes there was no money for coal, and my older brothers would have to go out to the back garden and find something that could be added to the fire.

They'd chop up old wood and whatever they could find, just to toss on the flames to generate some heat in the house for the evening.

Once my sister, Pat, and my mom were standing by the fire when bits of coal flew out of the fire and hit their legs. The hot ember made a little hole in Pat's leg.

I remember cold nights in the winter, when we just had candles instead of electricity because we had no money. At that time, we had to put a coin in the slot, either a ten pence or a six pence, to get electricity. Even with the black and white telly, we had to put a coin in the back to make it work.

Things weren't easy when I was a child, but we coped as best we could.

"Your dinner is on the table," Mom would say sometimes on Sunday, and we'd have lamb bones, just bones with some fat and a little bit of meat.

Then on Monday, going into Tuesday, we'd have the fat drippings on a piece of toasted bread for supper before bed.

We were always grateful for something to eat. One of our favorite meals was a sugar sandwich, which took the place of sweets. To this day, I don't eat sweets, perhaps because I didn't have them as a child.

In my flat in Chesterfield, at a time when there were articles about me in the news, I'd relax and meditate in the one room that never got warm. That's where I felt closest to the people I'd lost, as well as people from the past who had lived there. So many from the spirit world were with me.

Mary Desmond, a country western singer and writer, called me one day. "Tom, I've been reading so much about you and seeing your write-ups. Congratulations. Have you ever been to Ireland?"

I told her I had links to Ireland through my father's family, and had always wished to go. But I believe you've got to be guided, to be invited to different places.

Mary, who came across as very warm and loving, asked me to come to Ireland. She lived in the countryside outside the city of Cork, so we made arrangements for me to go there. Three months later I arrived at the airport, where Mary had arranged for some lovely people to meet me.

Soon, I was settled in a cottage in Cork, where she'd arranged for people to see me for healing and spiritual communication. She also arranged for me to talk about my work on the local Cork radio station.

Mary was the person who opened the door to Ireland for me, and I thanked her very much for that. I call Ireland my spiritual home, and I feel so close to my father when I'm there. As long as I continue working as a medium and healer, I'll always maintain a connection to Ireland and the people there.

Another Mary that I met soon after arriving in Cork had a niece who was a journalist at the local newspaper. The niece interviewed me about my work and my travels, and gave me a great write-up with colored photographs and pictures of me doing a healing.

After that, I approached the owner of a bookstore in St. Paul's Street. I told him I was a healer and medium, and asked if there was any chance he could let me use some space in the store for readings. Not only did he say yes, he provided space for me in his store a couple of days a week.

I loved working in Ireland, so I started traveling back and forth from London on a regular basis. At first, I kept doing my work in the area of Cork. I was on the radio station a few times, doing demonstrations of mediumship and healing, and received a great response.

Sometimes after I'd been to the bookstore, I'd drop by a little healing sanctuary on St. Paul's Street, located above a Burger King. Sometimes my friend Reg came along to do healing as well.

Ireland is a Catholic country, so I was taking small steps, but got to know the local people as I did my work.

For three and a half years, I traveled back and forth from Derbyshire to Ireland. I loved living in Derbyshire, but felt drawn to the people in Ireland.

Ireland felt like a calling for me, so I made a major decision to move. I left my little flat in Derbyshire, including all my furniture, kitchen stuff, cooker, fridge, bed, and everything else, and moved to a one-bedroom flat in Limerick, Ireland.

My most important inspiration to relocate was a little lady from Cork, a nun named Jenny, who I used to call "my angel." She told me "This is the place you should be helping people. You need to be closer to the people in need of your gifts."

As soon as I settled in, a lady called and asked me to do a healing for her son, a young man with cancer. He was only in his late thirties, but the doctors had told his parents he was going to die.

His mom knew there was only so much that could be done, but asked me to help because her son couldn't eat properly. Every time I arrived, his face would light up. He knew that after I'd put my hand on his chest where the pain was, he'd be able to eat his dinner for a few days. The family received peace of mind that their son was being helped, even in a small way. I was pleased that my guides and helpers from the spirit world were able to use me as an instrument of love.

Another time, I did an evening of clairvoyance in a little hall that was usually used as a bingo hall and social club. The owners agreed to let us do a demonstration for people reaching out, people who hoped they might be helped in some way. I went through the evening praying and sending healing in that little room, pulling people up front so I could put my hands on their heads or shoulders and pray for relief of pain, or stress.

My special friend, the little nun named Jenny, often went with me to watch my work. We traveled to different places throughout Ireland, even to Dublin.

On one occasion, Jenny and I worked together for a little ten-year-old boy who had trouble walking because of a bad left leg. Jenny and I first went to the church and said prayers, then went to the family's house. I reached out to the greatest spirit of all, and asked the guardian angels to come down from the spirit world to help the lad. The boy became able to stand up without pain, wonderful and inspiring.

By that time I was going to different parts of Southern Ireland, helping people in need to the best of my ability. Jenny, the little nun who helped and encouraged me so much, sent a letter to Pope John Paul and asked him to give me a blessing for the good work I'd done.

Receiving that card from the Pope brought tears to my eyes. I treasure it, and am so grateful to Jenny for doing that for me.

I have so many great memories of spending time with Jenny. We laughed for hours at the circus one time, just happy being together. Even though she was small, she had amazing strength and faith.

Sometimes I'd sit in the church, praying and attending the service with her. She'd invite me on walks with her and her niece, and we'd talk of spiritual things and about people reaching out with all their worries and stress. Other times we'd just sit and pray together.

Once while we were sitting down praying, I got a great inspiration. I started drawing a lovely little cross. Suddenly, words came into my mind while I was talking with Jenny and her niece. "Take the Lord Jesus home with you in your heart, and know that he's always walking with you hand-in-hand. God Bless, Tom Flynn."

We put the cross and words on a little card, and when I go to Ireland and do my healing, I give these out to people. They seem to enjoy taking these little texts home with them, and sometimes come back to me to tell me they still say those words.

One time, I was on a radio show with Jenny when a lad in a prison cell in Dublin phoned the station and asked me to send him some prayers. He was reaching out for help and guidance, so I tried to get to the prison to see him.

Jenny and I went to the gate, but were told we had to have more details and his prison number. We weren't able to see him, but continued sending out prayers to that young man.

I believe that whatever the circumstances, we should all reach out in our own way to help people, especially with a prayer.

In addition to our spiritual work together, Jenny was one of the few people I let help me with my writing and reading difficulties.

She'd sit and gently say, "Let's put some words down and see if you understand. I just want you to do some words."

She did this four or five times, sitting down and helping me. She'd even have a little book waiting for me to write in.

I believe in fate, and I know I was meant to meet that little nun so she could inspire me to overcome my learning problem.

She also shared her feelings about our Father, about guardian angels, and about the power of prayer. People come into our lives for some particular reason; even if just for friendship. Jenny was meant to be in my life to give me guidance and prayers of peace.

I knew Jenny for over two years before she passed into the world of spirit at eighty-nine years old. Losing someone like her is always hard, but we know that they live on in our memories. During a reading in 2003, my angel came through, and I was thrilled that Jenny still wanted to be close to me from the world of spirit.

Irish Connections

Some Dublin radio stations had me give healing and messages of hope on the air during a regular program for several weeks. The response was quite positive, so I was given a routine spot on their schedule. I was also interviewed on TV. The encouragement to continue working in Ireland was wonderful.

I found myself going to three different Irish hospitals, one in Limerick, one in Cork, and one in Dublin, where'd I'd pray for people in intensive care units.

In Dublin, a six-week-old baby boy had serious breathing problems. The doctors had told the parents that there was nothing more they could do. When the family asked for help, I put my hands over the baby, letting the spirit world use me as an instrument of love.

The family stood around the bed in silence, watching and praying, when they felt a cold sensation around them and their child. The baby made a dramatic recovery during the next four days. Two months later, I spoke to the family's auntie, and was told the boy was making great progress. I continued praying for him and sending distant healing.

I continued reaching out to people, and getting a little help from the press through articles published in Dublin and Cork. One time, I was doing an evening of healing at the Fitzpatrick Hotel in the Limerick area, with a large group of people suffering from a variety of pains.

One woman was suffering from cataracts. I put my hands across the woman's eyes, about six inches away from them. She said it felt like my fingers were going into her eyes, but that was from the spirits. Afterward, she could read without wearing her glasses. There's never a guarantee, but reaching out to people in the spirit world can bring incredible results.

I also did an evening of healing where near the home of Mary Desmond, the country western singer who'd first invited me to Ireland. I'd asked a radio station to run an ad, and to my amazement, about a hundred people turned up. I stood there for over four hours, laying my hands on what seemed like every single person there.

They were seeking healing for different reasons, such as the back, head, or stomach, so I aimed the spirit energy toward those areas.

In 2003, while I was in the Cary area with Phillip, a friend of mine, I received a phone call asking me to come to a hospital intensive care unit in Cork. Phillip drove me seventy miles from Cary to Cork to meet with the family, whose fifteen-year-old daughter had fallen off her pony.

The doctors were with the girl when I arrived. The family didn't know much about spiritual healing, but had heard of me and my work, so they put me up in a bed-and-breakfast near the hospital. The family had been told the doctors could not touch the brain of this young lady because of the blood rushing to it, so the priest was coming to give last rites.

Parents and friends were standing around when I walked in, shaking in my boots. I put my hand on the girl's head, keeping it there for about forty minutes. I told the family I would pray for their daughter to come back to them. My guides used me as an instrument of love, and I was successful.

Later, the girl had to go to Leeds in England for two facial operations, but is otherwise strong. When she asked to see the person who'd helped her, Phillip and I went to her house, where I gave another healing session. I phoned her on many occasions afterward, and believe she is progressing well.

As time went by, I was connecting with more and more people, and was the subject of another great article in Dublin. As a result of the publicity, I remained there in a hotel for about sixteen days, doing spiritual healing.

During one of the sessions, a guy having trouble with his back came to see me, but let me know he'd seen several different people looking for help. I told him there were no guarantees, but that I'd reach out to the spirit world to come through and help me.

As I was linking into the other side for the healing, he said he felt very relaxed and might fall asleep. After the session, he told me he'd been a sportsman and athlete before, and had even run marathons in London and America, but didn't know if he could do all that again. After telling me about his history, he asked about my fee.

I said, "I do this for love. I just ask for a donation of what you can afford."

About two weeks later he came back for a top-up, thanking me and saying his back felt really good.

I told him, "Don't thank me, thank God for using me to help you with this."

I started getting great results with slipped discs and curvature of the spine. Six months later, a lady called and asked, "Are you the man who's good with arthritis?"

That recommendation made me laugh. I sent out distant healing to her because she was so far away. Distant healing does work, and at the time I was also sending distant healing to a woman in Canada.

While I lived in Ireland and traveled back to London to work, I'd always stay with my friend Paul, in his flat. We've been friends since he helped me with reading after my parents died, and then through the years his parents welcomed and accepted me as one of the family. Being with Paul always brings back memories of my family, and reinforces my belief that my mom and dad are still guiding me.

Once during a regular radio spot in Limerick, between nine and ten in the morning, the father of a boy named

Tommy asked me to send prayers to him. We arranged to meet in person.

The family members were working to raise money for the boy to go to New York for an operation. I gave him healing seven or eight times, and his legs improved enough for him to walk about three or four consecutive steps before he got to America. In New York they called it a "Miracle on 34th Street. We heard that he got good results from the operation, but he also got a boost of help from the spirit world along the way.

While in Ireland, I used to go to church two times a week for about ten to fifteen minutes to pray for people all over the earth who needed help, asking for the highest spirits to help them. I'd put candles out, sit next to the angel of Jesus, and pray to Jesus Christ. I also used to go in Cork to a Saturday afternoon prayer service for people who were sick.

Kindred Spirits

I gave a reading to a very interesting man named Dennis McCarthy, whose father came through for him. Dennis said he'd like to see me again, so I invited him to come and watch a demonstration I was giving at the Victoria Hotel in Galway.

Dennis was full of life, fun, and good ideas, and also had gifts of healing and mediumship. I wanted to help him strengthen his abilities, so I took him along to some of my meetings.

I told him I'd give the service, the messages, and the healing. "All you have to do is sit back and tune in to the spirit world. If you have one message that night and help one person, you've served the spirit that night."

Dennis got stronger and more confident. We got together often, and would sit and do meditation, prayers, healings, and give one another healing as well. We also prayed for souls in the world who needed help. Wherever I am in the world, I continue to send healing to Dennis.

I was once asked by a lady to come to Dublin and do a charity event for children with cancer. She arranged the meeting place at a hotel in Dublin, set up the program, and then advertised the event on television and in the newspapers. About five hundred people turned up, making the event a fantastic success, and raising about 4,000 euros.

When I first stood in front of the crowd, I asked how many people had been to an event like mine before, and learned that for the great majority, this was a new experience.

I then asked how many were skeptic, and nearly all the hands went up. I was grateful no one walked out. The chap who collected the money for the charity asked if he could stay for ten minutes, but ended up staying for the entire two hours, so he must have enjoyed the clairvoyance and healing, too.

Once, while I was in Cary waiting for a demonstration to begin, I was surprised to see an Elvis Presley impersonator come into the building. I'd just been talking to him earlier in the day, and had no idea he was coming to see me. I gave him a message from someone special in the spirit world that, judging by his reaction, was a comfort to him. The spirit world calls back to their loved ones, using me as their instrument, their link, and feedback from the readings confirm the accuracy and love conveyed in the messages.

Providing a message for the Elvis Presley impersonator made me think of my own childhood. I remembered the fun I'd had singing and dancing, playing in the streets with the other children, and the love we shared in the family. I never would have imagined that I'd be living a life helping others with survival evidence and spiritual healing.

I did a half-hour radio program in Cork the day before doing a clairvoyant meeting. The meeting was also on the radio show, and to my shock over 200 people showed up. The person there helping me was overjoyed with the turnout, but I got very emotional and nervous before the program. I had to remind myself that I'd chosen to do the work, and that the spirit world is there not just for me, but also for other people who have questions.

When people ask me about my spirituality, I always tell them I'm a Christian, and then say a silent Lord's Prayer before doing healings. I always start each day and each event with a prayer for guidance.

During one of my stays in Cork, a lady came to me seeking comfort over the loss of her mother. She needed someone to listen to her express her feelings. We talked about twenty-five minutes, and then I sent healing vibrations in the colors of green and blue toward her.

After we talked, she said she felt so much better about the change we call death, and knew she could be stronger knowing her mother would always be close to her.

During my travels in Ireland, I also went to Belfast, in Northern Ireland. I stayed in the hotel where I was scheduled to do a demonstration, an evening of healing, and clairvoyance.

I met a great guy who ran a radio station there, who offered me an opportunity to promote the event on air. He set up a live linkup from the radio station to the hotel.

He started out by asking me how long I'd been doing this, and I answered "Over twenty years."

We had a great talk, bringing through lots of laughter and peace. I was so grateful for the messages, reinforcing once again that there is life after this world, and that we can join the two worlds.

A lady named Margaret called me requesting help for a young lad in the hospital. He had survived after jumping off a building, but had many broken bones throughout his body.

She asked me to go to the hospital and pray for him. When I arrived at the hospital I prayed for him, but I also put my hands around his leg area and gave a healing.

This young man survived through the great work of the hospital staff, and with a lot of love sent to him. We don't know what was in this lad's mind when he jumped, but we're glad he's still with us now.

Dennis McCarthy and I accepted a unique invitation to spend the night at a haunted castle. We traveled by train to join a group of twelve people, including the organizers of the group. We got to the castle at teatime, where we enjoyed talking with the group about their experiences at different haunted castles.

We stayed the night, and started investigating after midnight. We went into the cellar, which looked and felt more like a dungeon.

The members of the group wanted me to see if I sensed anybody. As I reached out to any spirits or people who'd dwelt there from the past, everyone focused their energy and love in my direction to assist me. I linked into the highest vibrations, the highest spirits from the spirit world, my helpers. I discovered that people had been put into the cellar to die. There had been eight meat hooks there, and people were hung up to die. The place was very airy and cold. We stayed in the cellar for a short while, and then walked outside. A couple of people in the group noticed white finger marks on my black top, and took pictures of them.

After spending several hours exploring, the group asked Dennis and me to spend the night in a bedroom that was said to be haunted. The stories say a lady appears and sits next to the dressing table, and then the bed moves. In fact, Fox TV in America sent a family to stay in the room, but those people couldn't do it. They tried, but ended up running out well before morning.

Dennis and I laid on top of the bed, fully clothed, because it was icy cold in the room, but slept like babies. After getting up in the morning, we went up on top of the carpark, where we both got a great feeling. People in the group were quite shocked when they developed two photographs they'd taken of Dennis and me standing on top of the carpark. The first one showed Dennis and me, but the next one showed a mist around me and a spirit light around Dennis. Dennis and I have copies of both pictures.

Another great time was on a St. Patrick's weekend. I was staying at the Victoria Hotel across the hallway from my usual room. I had changed rooms because my friend was coming, and we needed two beds. At 6:30 in the evening, I discovered there weren't enough towels in the bathroom for two men, and decided to tell the hotel staff.

About five minutes later I felt an unexplained pushing sensation on the door to the room. I opened it, and found two towels. I hadn't ordered them yet, so I went straight down to reception and asked the desk clerk if there was anyone else working at that time.

She said, "Only me and the barman in the bar."

I asked her if the cleaners worked late, but was told they'd gone at 4:30.

This just demonstrates the power of spirit. The story didn't end there. That night, Dennis and I visited a spiritual healer named Bill. Before I could tell him about my experience, he showed me a little buckle with a ship on it, and said it just appeared in his house. That made two strange physical manifestations in one day.

Many people who come to me want to develop their own gifts, and ask advice on the best way to find a teacher. I tell them that all workshops and development circles are different, and they must choose the one for them. The most important thing is feeling comfortable with that group and that teacher.

One special person I've been trying to help is my sister, Pat. Like most of our family members, she started getting visions as a young lady. For years she's felt connections with the spirit people in our family -- Mom, Dad, our two brothers, Michael and Raymond -- but her visions have been getting stronger.

I told her, as I tell others, to look inside herself and she will know where she wants to go with her gifts. I think she's ready to open the door to spiritually work to help others and to help herself.

America

In 2004, I gave a reading for Martina, a
lady living in Ireland. She was so
pleased because she received evidence
from loved ones who'd passed on that
they were in the spirit world, and could
still communicate with her.

Some time later, we met by
accident on the streets of Cork. We
ended up in a hotel drinking coffee,
having sandwiches, and talking more
about her first reading. In a Catholic
country like Ireland, Martina, like many
others, really wanted to know about the
spirit world first hand.

I was only too pleased to tell her
about my personal experiences of losing
my family to the spirit world, and how I
was guided through my Romany gypsy
mom and my Roman Catholic dad. I
explained to her that they were guiding
me forward from the spirit world. I
think she was overwhelmed to learn that
the spirit world was so close to her.

A short time later, I was astonished
when Martina's cousin Rose called me

from the United States. She lived in a San Francisco Bay Area town in California, and just wanted to talk.

For some reason, I started to connect with the spirit world and said, "I've got some messages coming through."

Often that happens, I'd be talking to someone on the phone, and messages would start flowing for me to share.

I described a man who had passed with a heart attack. Rose told me it was her brother, and then couldn't hold back her feelings. She started crying on the phone.

I said, "That's very natural. Let those feelings come."

Her mom and dad came through next, giving me descriptions of themselves, who they were, and why they were contacting Rose. They wanted her to know that they were still present in her day-to-day activities, and wanted to guide her and other family members forward.

The last messages that came through were from a couple of additional names that Rose didn't recognize, but later confirmed as family members.

After the personal messages, she asked me what my charge was for the reading, and I told her, "No, that's especially for you from your loved ones in the spirit world."

Just a few weeks later Rose called again, asking if I'd like to come to the San Francisco area. Great, I thought, and jumped at the opportunity. The funny thing was, just about two years prior I'd been asking to go to California. Proof again that the spirit world works in mysterious ways.

The trip was scheduled for February, 2004, and I was to stay with Rose's sister, Bernadette, in San Pablo. She welcomed me into her house for as long as I wanted to stay, and whenever I wanted to return to America, her doors were open to me.

I went back to San Pablo in 2005, and again stayed with Bernadette. She was taking her daughter and grandson to Disneyland for three days, and invited me to join them, fulfilling one of my biggest dreams.

Inside the Disneyland entrance was Steve Martin, who would become one of my favorite film stars. He worked there as a magician before he became famous.

We also went to the Disney California Adventure Park, directly across from Disneyland. To me, the greatest things of all were the fireworks and the Disney characters. There was no way to see everything in three days, but I'll always treasure my memories of Disneyland.

Bernadette and I also went to the cinema in San Jose to see *Mystic India*. That 45-minute film, the true story of an eleven-year-old boy's incredible, seven-year journey through India, moved me in ways I'd never expected.

My arms got very cold, and my eyes filled with tears. I knew this was one of my past lives. I know my spiritual journey will take me to India in the future, and I'm looking forward to meeting the people, and seeing some of the lovely places.

I've also wanted to go to Hawaii. I found some great travel deals, so I went for five days. I actually swam with the dolphins. The whole experience of Hawaii was unbelievable, walking and feeling the peace within. I'll always carry the memories of the wonderful atmosphere, standing at the beach, reaching out to the vibration of love, as I breathed the fresh air.

In America, I met a British lady, who was having tests in a hospital. I put my hands around the aura on her head, prepared to do a healing.

Suddenly she turned to me and said, "What about the spirits?"

I couldn't help but laugh. Here she was in the hospital, not well, and having tests, but she still wanted to talk to the people she'd loved. Her husband came through and told her he was always there for her. That was exactly the comforting message she needed, and her face lit up with joy.

From the Bay Area, I went to Sacramento, where I'd been invited by Rev. Sandra Dawson and her husband Robert, to serve at the Central Spiritualist Church. I served the church with prayer, talks, and clairvoyance, and have been back several times.

While in Sacramento, Peter, one of my new American friends, took me to the East West Bookstore. The bookstore, located in a suburb called Fair Oaks, had a comforting, peaceful atmosphere, so I asked if there was a chance for me to help people with spiritual healing.

Over a two-year period I got to know the bookstore quite well, and received help with doing the spiritual healing. I attended classes on guided meditation with a lady named Claudia, and also attended a class "Once a Month with the Masters" where spirit guides and angels came through from the spirit world.

Sacramento was the home of another amazing lady, Patricia Merrill, who used to sit next to me at the East West Bookstore. She was very down to earth, filled with kindness and encouragement. Patricia wrote about her spiritual growth in her book, *Autobiography of a British American Mystic*.

I saw her several times, including when she brought her daughter with her in November, 2006, for a healing. Patricia had a hereditary problem with her eyes, and had seen multiple doctors. She came for a healing and a little bit of comfort, which is exactly how it works. We reach out to the spirit world for comfort and healing vibrations from people we love.

Back in the Bay Area, I did a Sunday morning service at a little church in San Francisco. Reverend Wilma, a lovely little Scottish lady, welcomed me. After the service, several people traveled from the Bay Area up to the bookstore to see me for spiritual healing.

During my visit to the Bay Area in 2006, I had many people come see me for help and guidance from the spirit world. One young lady, named Karen, was amazed when her brother came through. He came through with a great deal of love toward her and their parents, lifting all their spirits.

What people need to realize, is that any time we wish to reach someone special to us on the other side, all we have to do is call their name, or bring through a memory about them, and they can be there with us.

During my visit in 2006, I also went to a hospital in Livermore to see a gentleman named Steve. Bernadette and Steve's sister, Nancy, came with me to give some spiritual healing. Steve had trouble breathing so I laid my hands on his. He told me he felt a lot better from the healing, and asked where my power came from.

I said to him, "From God."

Another place I wanted to visit in the United States was Las Vegas. Bernadette had business there, so I had the opportunity to spend three nights in the city. I'm not a gambler, but enjoyed the entertainment and looking at all the lights on the strip. We saw different shows each night, including two Elvis impersonators.

Before leaving for America in 2006, I'd talked about the trip to a lady I'd met in Ireland, who was thrilled because she had relatives living near where I was going. I was lucky enough to meet with her family and to bring back pictures for her. She was so excited to see the photographs, and to hear all about my meeting with them.

One time, while doing some spiritual healing at a church in the States, I met a guy named Kris, who invited me to Costa Rica. We went to a hotel there where people were ill. I was asked to give healing to a young man, about 18 years old, whose employer wouldn't let him lift things because of his sore back. I put my hands on his back, and he immediately felt a release of tension and pain.

The hotel manager invited me to stay for another two weeks to help other people with healings. I wasn't able to stay, but it was wonderful to be asked.

In Costa Rica, night, when all the insects come alive, there is a great atmosphere. Then when I woke in the morning, I could hear the monkeys carrying on and jumping through the branches.

The Islands of Costa Rica are so peaceful, with lovely beaches, trees, and a feeling of calmness like Hawaii.

As a child, I'd dreamed of different places, wondering what it would be like, and now it was coming together like a jigsaw puzzle. When I lost my mom and dad, I didn't know what was going to happen to me, but I tried to stay levelheaded to the best of my ability, even though I sometimes struggled, as with reading and writing.

I kept on pushing, refusing to give in. I was very determined, maybe a bit stubborn, really. My brothers and sisters kept me straight, making sure I knew right from wrong. I kept on going forward, enjoying life, and pushing myself. How marvelous to have people guiding me.

All my friends were on the right path forward, leading me with them in strength, courage and determination. When I worked as a baker, it gave me independence, and taught me it was possible to rise above struggles.

I've always loved singing, and sometimes during an evening of clairvoyance, while I passed on spiritual messages, I'd get the memory of a song. And there I'd be, standing up on the platform singing away, a song that was a memory of someone from the spirit world, hoping it meant something to someone in the audience.

Sure enough, a hand would go up, and I could see that person's eyes light up with the love of the music and the connection they had with someone on the other side that loved that song.

Working with the spirits has given me confidence, as well as pleasure. I want to be with them as long as they want me to be. Sometimes I've done three churches in a night for the sheer joy of it. Love and laughter are two of the best parts of my work.

Music has always been a special part of my life. Looking back, the music of the '60s, '70s, and '80s were big influences on my brothers and me. We all had different styles of dress, based in part on what kind of music we preferred.

I had long hair, and used to wear orange trousers, orange tee shirts, and blue shirts with white stars. My second eldest brother, Dannie, and brother Mickey were rockers, and used to wear leather jackets and greased-back hair. My brother, Raymond, who passed in a house fire, wore a suit and short hair.

Dannie knew famous pop stars, The Dave Clark Five. They used to play with my brother on our street, Strawberry Road. I believe Mike Smith and the others used to live in Upper

Edmonton. Mike Smith used to show up on the street to play with my brothers, and come into our house and say hello to my mom. I can imagine my mom giving them six pence to go round to the shops. In time, they lost contact, but I still have great memories.

During my first visit to America, I went with Bernadette to see Herman and the Hermits on the Fourth of July. They were singing in a park. The lead singer, Peter Noone, was asking people to send prayers to Mike Smith, who had been in an accident and was in the hospital. I sent healing prayers to him, as did loads of other people.

The people I've met spiritually in my work have helped me gain confidence to continue going forward. Nothing has stopped me from continuing to progress, even when I was twenty-one and started having grand mal seizures. My mom and dad have continued giving me love from the spirit world so I can help people.

Spiritual understanding gives so much peace of mind. It changed me. I never used to go for walks. I didn't care about strolling by the sea. I was not drawn to quiet places. But now I love nature, and enjoy all of those things.

Sometimes, when I'm with people who aren't into spirituality, they'll ask lots of questions about what I do. I tell them I just sit there and ask the great spirit of the universe to shine on us, so that I can give messages of truth and peace to people.

I remember watching a medium in Chesterfield who did trance work. He called out, "Is there a Tom Flynn here?"

He went on to tell me he saw travel in Europe, Ireland, and America for me. All of those things have opened up for me over the years. I can't run. I can only take small steps doing the work I do. Slowly the doors have opened for me. But I've always came back to London, my home.

Instrument of Love

I have great memories of the churches I've
served, and have enjoyed every minute of
it. When I'm in London, I still like to sit
in the local Spiritualist Church, at the
Edmonton Spiritualist Church in
Edmonton, or at the Beacon of Light
Church in Enfield. It's such a pleasure just
to sit there and feel the love and peace,
and to listen to the speakers. I always send
out great vibrations of love to everyone,
especially those receiving spiritual
messages.

Another of my favorites in the
London area is The Woodgreen
Spiritualist Church, a warm and
welcoming place I'm always eager to
revisit. I've often done Wednesday night
services there, and remember the church
president, Mrs. Ida Stenning, cheering me
on every time. She has passed to the spirit
world where I'm sure she was welcomed
with open arms as a great ambassador for
the spiritual movement.

I've met so many nice people on my
spiritual journey. I hope I will continue to
meet people of like mind, to give them
guidance and the knowledge that there is

111

proof of life after death. I pray that spirit will continue to use me as an instrument of love to help people.

PART TWO
More About Tom
By
Sharon S Darrow

Reading Tom's words is inspiring and infectious, but they only tell half the story, while raising a lot of questions. How did a man in London end up working with an author in California? Did Tom's readings make lasting changes in people's lives? What do some of Tom's friends say about him?

Kris Machalica

I've never believed in coincidences. In fact, one of my favorite sayings has always been

Coincidences are small miracles
where God prefers to remain anonymous.
Author unknown

But now I have a much better description for what looks like impossible coincidences. Vivienne Brocklehurst, who has been friends with Tom for many years, calls them "Spirit Planning." This book is a perfect example.

Kris Machalica, one of Tom's closest friends, saw a social media posting about an NCPA (Northern California Publishers & Authors) meeting that said guests were welcome. When he arrived at the location, Cool River Pizza in Roseville, California, Kris sat in his car for about ten minutes, listening to heavy rain beat down on his roof, before working up enough courage to go inside. He was sure no one would talk to him or be interested in what he had to say, but his determination to help Tom drove him forward.

As President of the NCPA, I always watch for new faces at meetings, so when Kris sat down close to me, I welcomed him and introduced myself. Kris told me he wasn't a writer, but was trying to help his friend in London get his book published.

In his hands, Kris held a yellow, spiral-bound notebook. Tom's book consisted of transcribed pages from audiotapes Tom had recorded in 2006. Kris and I agreed that he'd email a copy of the manuscript for me to review, so I could suggest an editor suitable for the material.

That very evening, I started reading, but the first ten pages or so didn't tell me anything other than the fact that this manuscript was not ready for an editor. In fact, I hadn't been able to figure out what it was about. But Kris had made such an impression on me that turning my back on the project just didn't feel right, so I called him with lots of questions.

When I learned about Tom and what he does, I was hooked. I'm not a medium like Tom, but I am an intuitive, and have been dealing with the spirit world for decades. I knew right away that I didn't want to pass Tom on to an editor; I wanted the opportunity to write the book for him and get it published.

Kris explained that he was talking on Tom's behalf, and would be his local contact. Tom often traveled around the world, which made it difficult to stay in touch with him. Since Kris and I both understood we needed to know each other better if we might be working together, we made an appointment to meet and talk.

My first question was why Tom's transcribed audiotapes had been sitting around for ten years. Kris explained Tom had been encouraged to do a book about his life, but didn't know where or how to start. He was pursuaded to make the audiotapes, which a friend then transcribed. The next step, getting the material edited and put into proper manuscript format, had been the problem. Years went by, with one potential writer expressing interest at first, but then backing out because of discomfort with the subject matter. Then when Kris tried to find a publisher to handle everything, he discovered how many predatory publishers are in the market these days, offering incredible promises in return for huge upfront fees.

My next questions were about how Kris's friendship with Tom had come about, and why he was so willing to help Tom. Here are Kris's own words about their history together.

Tom is a dear and special friend. I received a healing from him in 2005, during a service at a Spiritualist Church in Sacramento. I was immediately impressed by the energy he transferred, and invited him to my house for a reading. We spent a few hours getting to know each other, and I'm proud to say, we've been close friends ever since.

Talking to Tom and being around him has helped me understand so much more about Spiritualism. I've seen Tom working with people, healing and helping communicate with loved ones in the spirit world. He's great at what he does, because he works from the purest intentions, from his huge heart.

Tom's always there for me, ready with a helping hand and kind words. He brightens my days with wise comments and his great sense of humor.

I've traveled with Tom in his home country as well as exotic places, and he's a great travel companion. Tom's always so gentle and open people, loving and caring. It's been a true joy to experience many great adventures together.

Kris (on left) and Tom (on right)
relaxing in Costa Rica

I believe through people like Tom and their special gifts, we can spread awareness about Spiritualism and continuation of life after death. His work of touching hearts and souls opens many people to the concepts of religion, science and philosophy, which comprise Spiritualism."

Kris liked the idea of Tom and me as co-writers -- his story, my writing -- and that I'd handle the process of getting the book published. We were eager for the next time Kris could bring Tom to Sacramento for the three of us to work out the details.

After deciding on our next steps, Kris and I started talking more about ourselves. Kris had owned a print shop, and done business with my family's laminating and index-tab business before it closed in 2008. Every single day I'd driven past his shop on the way to work. He thought the world of my mom, June Azevedo, and was thrilled at the idea of getting back in touch with her. We also learned that the little Spiritualist Church where he'd met Tom was less than a mile from my house.

The two of us were amazed at all the coincidences that brought us together for what seemed like a perfect match. The last step was for me to give Kris a copy of my book, *From Hindsight to Insight, A Traditional to Metaphysical Memoir*, so that he and Tom could learn more about me, and about what type of writer I am. I felt they needed to know me well enough to have confidence in me as a person, as well as a writer. Would my writing style be right for Tom's story?

Teresa Klimek

When I first met Tom, right after he and Kris returned from a month in Costa Rica, I understood why people were so drawn to him. My initial impression was of warmth, intelligence, and kindness. He exhudes a wonderful, almost childlike feeling, utterly without guile, as if he hasn't a deceitful bone in his body.

Kris's very dear friend, Teresa Klimek, does a great job describing what meeting Tom is like, and how he can change one's life.

I'd heard a lot about Tom from my friend Kris, and was anxious to meet him, even though I'd always considered myself a non-believer. Perhaps a better description would be to say I was a skeptic when it came to religions, life after death, and things like that. All of those beliefs changed when I had a chance to see Tom doing the service at a Spiritualist Church in Sacramento.

There were about 30 people in church that day, all strangers to Tom except for Kris and me. When Tom started doing his readings, I felt my jaw drop, right along with every person he read for. His messages were so accurate, some of the people cried. I couldn't believe my eyes and ears. I broke out in goose bumps. It was one of the most amazing experiences of my life.

Tom and I became instant friends the first day we met. He's a warm and good-hearted person, a pure soul. Tom's an open minded man, who seems to want to spend his life helping others in whatever way he can. He's like an angel, without a bad bone in his body. To talk to Tom for only a moment changes people to want to be around him all the time. To enjoy the warmth and caring you felt while in his presence.

I never would have imagined it possible, but Tom has made me an absolute believer in life after passing. It's changed me in many ways, since my life now has more meaning, knowing that there's much more than just what we can see and touch on Earth.

I wish everyone could meet Tom or someone like him. Since Tom and I became friends, my life is so much richer and has more meaning.

Thank you, Tom!

I learned from talking with Tom and reading through his transcripts how important his family was to him. Tom's relationship with his parents was one of the key influences in his life -- the loving influence of his parents, the unbelievable pain when they died so young, the incredible joy of having their continued presence and support as spirit guides.

Tom's parents,
Dennis and Genty Flynn

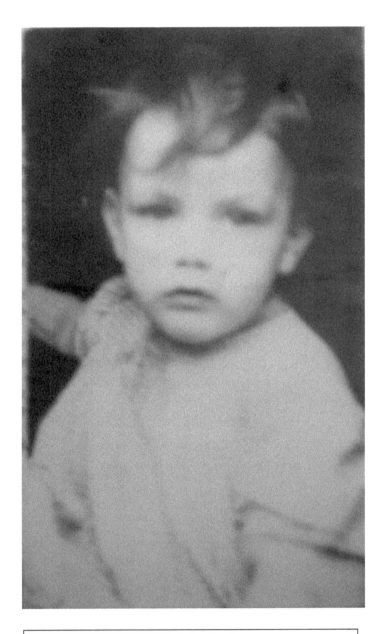

Tom as a one-year-old baby

Spiritualism

Many of Tom's family members were psychic, including his Aunt Mary, who was a medium and healer. Mary pushed Tom into doing his first readings, but the Spiritualist Churches soon became the most common venues for his work.

I've known about mediums and healers long before starting on Tom's project, but nothing about Spiritualist Churches. The quickest, easiest way to learn was to attend a service at the Central Spiritualist Church, the one near my home where Kris and Tom had met. Parts of the service were familiar -- the pastor lead prayers, the congregation sang hymns, and the had a call for offerings. However, some things were new to me. I'd never before seen healers and mediums as part of a regular church service. I was quite intrigued when everyone read the NSAC (National Spiritualist Association of Churches) Declaration of Principles printed inside the hymnals:

1   We believe in Infinite Intelligence.

2   We believe that the phenomena of Nature, both physical and spiritual, are the expression of Infinite Intelligence.

3   We affirm that a correct understanding of such expression and living in accordance therewith, constitute true religion.

4   We affirm that the existence and personal identity of the individual continue after the change called death.

5   We affirm that communication with the so-called dead is a fact, scientifically proven by the phenomena of Spiritualism.

6   We believe that the highest morality is contained in the Golden Rule: "Do unto others as you would have them do unto you."

7   We affirm the moral responsibility of individuals, and that we make our own happiness or unhappiness as we obey or disobey Nature's physical and spiritual laws.

8   We affirm that the doorway to reformation is never closed against any soul here or hereafter.

9   We affirm that the precepts of Prophecy and Healing are Divine attributes proven through Mediumship.

The nine statements seemed so straightforward to me, and so in line with my own beliefs. I was amazed to find a place that felt so much like home. I was even more amazed to learn that every individual Spiritualist Church Tom named in this book is still active today.

The Central Spiritualist Church where Tom and Kris met is also the place where I watched Tom give readings at a service. He was so relaxed, so comfortable with everyone. I have met mediums before and heard readings, but I was shocked by the specific details of Tom's readings. He told one person that his mother was a bit irritated with him for leaving the kitchen messy when he left for church, saying he could have at least dumped out the cup of coffee and rinsed it instead of leaving it on the counter.

Another Spiritualist Church in California where Tom is a regular visitor is the Golden Gate Spiritualist Church in San Francisco. I attended a service in the hopes of learning more about Tom and the people who know him. That church is as warm and friendly as the tiny one I visited in Sacramento. The building, however, is an awe-inspiring mansion in the heart of San Francisco.

Every year Tom spends a few weeks in California, staying with his many friends in the San Francisco Bay Area. Each person I've met was happy to share stories about him, and how much he has come to mean to them.

Tom giving a reading at the Central Spiritualist
Church, in Sacramento, California

Karen Zeppa

Karen Zeppa often hosts Tom when he comes to the Bay Area. Here are several of her remarkable stories in her own words.

Tom was a friend of a friend of a friend of a friend when I met him in 2006. I had tragically lost my beloved brother Steve, who died in a terrible tractor accident at the age of 52. Steve had retired in March, 2003, after serving as a Richmond police officer for 30 years, and died just six months later. His death was the worst possible pain I'd ever experienced.

I thought, I know life's unfair, but really? After surviving Richmond, one of the worst areas crimewise in the whole San Francisco Bay Area? Steve was in San Ramon, just getting ready to enjoy his life. He was planning a trip to Italy, and a kitchen- remodeling project, when tragedy struck.

Retired police officers think they're immortal after surviving so much on the job, and are often kind of addicted to adrenaline, too. Steve was riding a tractor over a steep road, helping a friend pave a road in Alamo, when the tractor went over the side. Steve fell off and got the wind knocked out of him. The fireman who responded, since the paramedics couldn't get there in time,

131

gave him a tracheotomy and one of my brother's lungs collapsed. He was without oxygen for longer than fifteen minutes. Steve was taken to the hospital, where he remained in a coma for nine days. We all visited and talked to him since we were told that he could hear us, but he didn't recover.

After Steve died I was beside myself with grief. Thank God I have a private cottage I could work out of, and clients who understood what was happening. I'd break down every now and then and just cry. I thought the tears would never stop. I've always been open to the belief system that souls survive death and communicate with their loved ones, but I'd never had a first-hand experience. Then my friend Nancy, who knew my brother had died but didn't know any of the details, recommended Tom. Her daughter had a friend of a friend that knew him, and he happened to be close by in San Pablo.

Have you ever opened a book and put your finger on a paragraph to get a quick message? This is what happened to me while I was trying to get up my courage to contact Tom. I'm not a Bible thumper by any means, but I was really nervous about getting a reading from a medium. I opened up the Bible and put my finger right on Corinthians 13, which says, "he who has the gift of spirit and prophecy is nothing if not charitable."

I called Tom, and found him to be such a joyful person when we talked on the phone, with *that cute little accent of his. My fears disappeared. He was so jovial and lovable, not at all like one of those spooky mediums you think are out there.*

Tom started the reading by first reading my aura, the colors around me, and knew that my favorite color is green.

He also told me I'm a healer, which is true. I do hair and also do healing.

Then Tom said, "Hmm, there's a man here, and he has something to do with the month of June."

I said, "Well, my brother's birthday's in June." I didn't tell Tom he was deceased. I knew better than to give any specific information, or as they say, "Don't feed the medium!"

Then Tom goes, "He was a very emotional man, he's showing me he was grieving. He's showing me a picture of a large tractor-like vehicle skidding off the side of a country road."

All the blood rushed out of my face. I thought, Oh my God, my God.

Tom told me the details of the accident, but said not to worry about Steve, because he left his body really fast, and didn't suffer. He told me what happened when I saw my brother for the last time at the hospital, repeating what I said verbatim.

"I'll always have you in my heart, it's okay to go home, I love you." the exact words I'd used. Then Tom told me Steve was kissing me on the

right side of the forehead, which is precisely what I'd done after telling my brother goodbye.

I was blown away at how accurate Tom was, and the tears started flowing as if floodgates had opened. I felt like my brother was in a good place, and was at peace.

Steve would have liked Tom. My brother used to sense the presence of spirits near the bodies he encountered on the job, and knew there was something there. He often told fellow police officers that he could feel "something else, out there."

After the reading, when I was able to calm down, Tom asked me what there was to do around here. The only thing he had going on was taking the train to Sacramento, where he'd do readings at the East West Bookstore, a metaphysical bookstore in Sacramento.

I said, "You know what, I'm going to turn you on to some clients, a whole group of people who would love to get a reading from you."

That was the start of what has become a lifelong friendship. I started hosting him whenever he came to the Bay Area, but had to be very discrete whom I told, because some people would think I was crazy.

My sister-in-law and Steve were like a tag comedy team. She'd open her computer and find a big smiling face there "by accident" and start laughing. She knew it was Steve, reminding her of his big, goofy grin.

She enjoyed Tom coming to her home, and didn't say anything when he'd start walking through the house. One day he took her right to a closet that contained a lot of Steve's tools that had been used in the kitchen during the remodel.

Tom said, "Let your brother have the tools, Steve doesn't care."

Then Tom took her to the bedroom, pointed at two drawers, and said, "These drawers are filled with his T-shirts. Get rid of them. Don't hang on to them."

Sure enough, the drawers were full of Steve's shirts. Tom also helped her find a ring that she'd thought one of the construction workers had taken.

Another time when Tom was staying with me, I was planning an 80th birthday party for my dad at the Galileo Club in Richmond. I invited Tom to go with me to get some things at my dad's house, particularly some pictures of him when he played sports. The plan was to blow them up for wall decorations at his party.

I'd told Dad that Tom was coming to the party, and that he was a medium and might give a reading. While I was fixing them lunch at Dad's house, Tom suddenly hopped up and started pacing the length of the house.

He said, "He's not going to let me finish me bloody lunch. We've got your son here, Al. Were you up all night crying because you regretted not spending enough time with him when he was a child?"

Tears in his eyes, Dad said, "Yeah, I was so selfish. I was always playing sports when I should have spent time with him."

Tom said, "You've got to stop that. You bonded over sports when you guys were adults."

Then Tom led us to a back bedroom where there was a box containing some of Steve's belongings. He opened up a box full of signed baseballs that Steve had collected during the time he'd gone to baseball games with Dad at PacBell Park.

Tom said, "You need to lay that to rest and not feel guilty. You guys bonded as adults. He's giving you a big hug, and he'll be there at your birthday party."

Dad was in tears, but it was an incredibly healing experience for him."

Karen and I talked a second time, when she was able to share more stories, including testimony about Siri, the voice on Apple products, and Franklin Delano Roosevelt.

I tried to get Tom a mini-iPad because he has a hard time spelling words. I thought it would be great for him, since he could talk into it in full sentences for posting on FaceBook and whatnot. But there's a learning curve with his accent.

We were in my dining room when Tom decided to post something healing to Billy the dog, which was picked up by Siri as, "I want to talk to Mark, Tom." My husband Mark's dad was deceased before he was even born, but how would it go from "something healing to Billy the dog" to "I want to talk to Mark, Tom."

Tom and I both freaked out, so we said, "Okay Dad, if this is you, give us a sign."

My dad and I used to go to the racetrack and ask my deceased brother, "Okay Steve, what's the winning horse at the racetrack?" So I said, "Okay Dad, what's the winning horse at the racetrack?"

And Siri spelled out "Dominique," which was Mark's Dad's middle name.

The story about FDR, Franklin Delano Roosevelt, is even stranger. Tom did a group reading at my cousins, Roberta and Mary's house in Livermore. About twelve women were there, not one of whom had ever laid eyes on Tom before. They didn't know who he was, and he didn't know them. First, Tom went around the room giving mini-messages to everyone, nothing too personal though, since it was public.

Then, he went up to Pam, and said, "You feel a little draft around your feet. I'm seeing a little black scottie dog running around down there."

The blood rushed out of Pam's face, and she said, "Go on, go on."

Tom continue. "And he brings with him a President. This President is very proud and upright. He wants to thank you for the work you do commemorating him."

Pam is a docent tour guide on the USS Potomac, in Jack London Square. The ship had been known as FDR's floating white house,.

Then Tom said, "And Elvis never lived there."

Tom had no way of knowing that Elvis Presley bought the USS Potomac after FDR passed away, but never lived on it. Pam just sat there, flabbergasted and not saying anything, listening to Tom's every word.

And then Tom said, "And he was a Spiritualist."

Nobody knew that since it wasn't something that FDR had shared with the public. But Rev. Dale Lauderback, pastor at Golden Gate Spiritualist Church, confirmed the information for me. FDR was almost best friends with the founder of the Golden Gate Spiritualist Church, Rev. Florence Becker. He not only got readings from her, he used to fly her to the White House for advise during World War II.

After that incredible reading, Pam invited Tom aboard the USS Potomac for a tour, to see what he'd pick up. As soon as Tom stepped on board, he walked straight to FDR's office and sat down. When he tried to stand up, he said, "I can't feel my legs. My legs have given out from under me."

Tom had no clue about FDR's lameness, but picked it up immediately.

Tom doesn't read for me much anymore, because we're so close. But I got a reading from

*him after my first interview for this book.
October is always a hard month for me, since
that's the month my brother passed. On October
20th, the anniversary of Steve's accident, I was
feeling very emotional while setting things up in
my cottage for work, when Tom came in.*

*"Guess who's here," he said, "Your mom's here
and she wants to give you a big hug. She knows
it's a hard day for you. She's holding Steve's
hand, and together they're giving you a hug."*

*Now it's 2016, I've known Tom for ten
years and introduced him to most of my clients.
About 90% of them have had readings with Tom
and learned to love him.*

Barbara

Barbara is another interesting person who's been a friend of Tom's since he first visited the Golden Gate Spiritualist Church. She's been attending the church for about fifteen years, and has served in various capacities, including Church Secretary. In addition to serving the church in whatever way she can, Barbara is always ready to help visitors, whether they're attending for the first time, or, like Tom, who've come to serve. Here is her story of their friendship.

I was one of the church workers when Tom came for the first time. He appeared nervous, but looked directly in my eyes and said, "You pray a lot, don't you."

I'm constantly praying in my mind, praying, praying, praying, so for him to pick that up was pretty cool. He earned some points from me for that. We became friends right away, and hung out together while he was here. He never did readings for me, probably because we were so close. Tom's also a healer, but because of our closeness, he was unable to help me with my back pain. I understand that messages don't always come through, and I have no problem accepting that. I always feel close to spirits, can sense them around me, but don't feel a necessity to talk to them or receive messages.

I've met many fine mediums at the church, but Tom is the best by far. I love it when he gives details like names, belt and shoe sizes. I've heard him describe the clothing the spirits wore while they were living, and what they passed from. Tom often provides information about what the spirits liked to do in life, even how they laughed. Only someone who is truly getting messages from the spirit world could provide those types of details. Best of all, Tom always gives the information with humor and compassion, even though the person receiving it often ends up crying.

If I had to describe Tom to someone who hadn't met him, I'd say he's joyful and genuine. He never puts on any airs, nor tries to be someone other than who he is. Sometimes Tom is very playful, and people don't quite know how to take him. He never "puts on a show" when he's doing readings, but his British sense of humor is lovely.

I feel very protective of Tom because I love him. Sometimes I get upset when people say something about him, but he doesn't let other people's remarks worry him. Tom could charge a lot more for his readings, like some of the famous mediums out there, but he hardly charges anything. Often he'll reduce his price if the person he's reading for can't afford it. Tom is just a good, generous man. I've told him that the good he does for other people will come back to him, and it does, over and over.

I'm very proud of the fact that I helped Tom do his very first workshop at the church. He charged less than anybody else does for workshops, but everyone who attended got a lot out of it. I did all the promotion for the event, and was very pleased with the outcome.

I was living with my aunt, taking care of her when Tom and I first met and became close. He would go with me back to my aunt's to take care of the dog, and then we'd just hang out together. Tom and I both love to eat, to go walking with the dog, and attend different kinds of shows. We also love karaoke with friends from church. Tom's quite the singer. He's also an ardent sports fan, and talks a lot about soccer. Tom knows all about the different teams, pays close attention to the games, and loves to wear sports jerseys.

My aunt passed while Tom was here, and it was very traumatic. She was living in a care facility at that time. I wasn't happy with the care she was receiving from the staff, and had tried to advocate on her behalf. My attempts resulted in my being banned from the facility.

Tom would visit her every day, while I waited in the car. On what turned out to be the very last visit, our dog wanted to go inside, too, so Tom took it with him. He also took my aunt some of her favorite snacks and treats, while I remained outside in the car. She loved Tom, and passed during the night shortly after Tom had visited with her.

My aunt's passing was sudden and unexpected, and I was devastated. Tom stayed with me every step of the way, going to the funeral parlor and supporting me as I made all the arrangements. He watched out for me, taking me to dinner and making sure I took care of myself. I believe that God brought Tom here at exactly the right time to help me through my grief. Without him, I would have been all alone.

Tom even spoke at my aunt's funeral, reminding everyone what a wonderful, beautiful soul she was. I know she was there watching him, and was pleased.

David M. Baker

Tom has many, many friends in the San Francisco Bay Area, and not all of them were from the Spiritualist Churches. One of them is his good friend and staunch supporter, David M. Baker. David is also a well known psychic and medium, and does a great job talking about himself and his relationship with Tom.

I was born with the gift of precognition and the ability to see and communicate with ghosts and crossed over spirits. I also have the ability as a healer. I have done all of the above. My main preference, though, is as a practicing medium. I always knew I had the gift and started testing and studying it in 1969 until 1972 and didn't do anything more with it until the late 1990s. After my father's death in 2005 I decided to go all in with my abilities. I wrote a book about my experiences in 2006 and published it in April of 2007.

Since 2006, and until 2009, I had a booth at the "New Living Expo" in San Francisco, California, where I did readings, lectures on stage and promoted my book "The Spirit Garden, a Medium's Journey." During the 2007 event at the "NLE" where I was at my booth, a client came in for a reading. I gave that gentleman a reading with good and validated information, both psychic and medium. I brought through his deceased father, a well-known healer, and gave other messages.

Then the client introduced himself to me. "David, do you know who I am? I am Tom Flynn a medium."

I said yes I have heard of you. Then he asked if he could give me a reading and I agreed. While I do not remember most of the details of the reading, I remember that he gave me a very detailed reading. I was thinking this man is awesome; his reading to me was amazing! What a gifted medium. His reading stunned me and I knew that I had just met a highly gifted person, even better than myself! I could tell he was well experienced and that he never struggled to bring forth any information.

Since that day, we formed a great friendship and stayed in contact. I have worked with him and witnessed his readings before a crowd, time after time, and he delivered very accurate messages. I have seen people that he read for both with smiles and tears. Although I was already a medium, I took courses on mediumship just to perfect my skills. In those courses, we were told that you know when a medium gives an authentic and great reading, when you see the sitter (person receiving the reading), is in tears. I have often witnessed that with Tom.

I have done video interviews with Tom Flynn and a few shows with him as my guest on my radio show "Beyond the Gate." Whenever he was a guest, we would take callers from all around the United States, and the world, and he'd answer questions and give amazing readings. He is a very popular guest, as our switchboard would always light up to capacity. I have witnessed him in action and not only are his abilities extraordinary, but he is a very humble man, never taking credit for himself.

As a well-traveled medium, author, speaker, teacher in this field and radio host, I know and have met many of the world's top mediums like Lisa Williams, James Van Praagh, John Holland, Derek Acorah, Terry and Linda Jamison (The Psychic Twins), Michelle Whitedove, Silvia Browne, Echo Bodine, Chip Coffey and more, and I include Tom Flynn among the ranks of these great top mediums and healers.

Vivienne Brocklehurst

Tom has friends all over the world, but his heart belongs to his home in the United Kingdom. One of his oldest and dearest friends is Vivienne Brocklehurst, who still lives in Chesterfield where they met, and who graciously shared the story of their friendship with me.

I first learned about Tom Flynn through articles I read in the Psychic News. I'd been reading the paper for years, and had also had some of my stories published in it. One day, in 1996, I saw a piece in the Psychic News that said Tom was leaving London and coming to live in Chesterfield. I rang his new number, which had been published in the story, and invited him to join the Chesterfield Psychic Study Group, which met at the town's community center. To our delight, he became a vital member of the group, which is still active and thriving today.

Tom's healing, intercessions, and clairvoyant readings were memorable contributions to the meetings. He always let people know that he could never guarantee that healing would take place before calling on spirit for assistance. It was more difficult for him to do readings and healings for close friends, although sometimes he helped with chronic pain. During one of the gatherings, a member, Jean Jackson, came with a badly swollen leg, which had been injured in a minor car accident. She requested a healing from Tom, and I closed my eyes to help during Tom's healings, just as I always did. Suddenly I heard all the group members say, "Oh." Opening my eyes, I saw that Tom, guided by his spirit healer, Dr. Eisenberg, had cured the swelling on Jean's leg.

On another occasion, while giving flower readings, Tom told a man that he was going to a musical concert. The message was not accepted. After awhile, the man's wife said, "You're right. We had planned to take him to a musical concert on his birthday, but it was supposed to be a secret."

Tom also received interesting information from other mediums during our meetings. Les Driver, a famous trance medium, told Tom that when he was a baby, his mother used to push him in his pram to visit the famous healer, Ted Fricker.

Tom has now returned to the London area after serving churches up North. He's been seen on platforms in Sheffield, Chesterfield, Doncaster, Mansfield, Darley Dale, and at Grassmoor Psychic Centre. Now Tom's horizons stretch far and wide. He's become an international medium, promoting Spiritualism across the globe.

Due to chronic rheumatoid arthritis, I've been housebound for many years, but Tom calls me from all over the world. It's been so exciting to hear his voice from America, Australia, Canada, Tenerife, the Caribbean Islands, and even from Hawaii in the Pacific Ocean.

Grieving people in the thousands need the reassurance of an after life in spiritual dimensions. They need to hear that death isn't the end, it's just a progression. It's going home. We're only temporarily separated from loved ones, whether they are family, friends or pets. In a world where news bulletins are about terrorism, disasters, accidents and destruction, Tom gives hope to people with whom he comes into contact.

Newspaper Articles

Tom's career as a medium started in a Spiritualist Church, and he continued offering services in them, so it's no surprise that articles about him began appearing in the Psychic News.

The Psychic News is now a magazine, available in both print and internet versions, with subscribers around the world. As Tom started gaining followers, stories began appearing about him. The magazine staff is still supportive of Tom, including taking the time to send several articles that had been published about him through the early years.

Tom Flynn's List Of Healing Help Grows

I t was during a psychic study group in Chesterfield last March that Joan Horvath met the medium and healer Tom Flynn.

Joan asked Tom whether he would consider coming to her home to give healing if she could get a group of people together.

Tom kept his word and a year on (this March) he was at Joan's home bringing in his guides and helpers.

Tom came to a lady present in the group Maureen Hill who claims she only came to escort her son-in-law, Vic Hill.

"The spirits have chosen you," Tom told Maureen.

Now Maureen confessed that for over three years she has been suffering from severe pain in her right shoulder and has sciatica in

Medium and healer Tom Flynn

her spine which the doctors have told her she must live with and continue to take pain killers for the rest of her life.

Tom told Maureen that she was now having psychic surgery performed on her shoulder and neck glands by his guide Dr Eisenburg and his Chinese surgeon.

Suddenly Maureen cried, "It's just magic. I've lost all my pain everywhere in my body and really should have been wearing my collar."

"What was the pink tablet you took last night?", Dr Eisenburg asked Maureen.

"I could not sleep because of the pain, so I took one of Vic's pink tablets to try and ease the pain and help me to sleep," replied Maureen who kept on that she only here to accompany her son-in-law Vic.

"Don't take any more pink tablets from this day on, because you have now been healed," instructed Dr Eisenburg.

The next person the spirits had selected was stroke victim, Frank Shaw who had first met Tom Flynn through Joan Horvath last July the time Frank was paralysed in his left hand and leg and unable to go to the toilet or walk without assistance.

Frank has since had eight sessions of healing with Tom Flynn either at Joan's flat or Joan would arrange for Frank to visit Tom's flat.

Frank Shaw can now hold a cup and has a drink without any help and can even use the toilet on his own.

"The world of spirit are wonderful,

and every time he receives healing from Tom and his guides this really does help Frank to get better,' says Joan Horvath.

Vic Price was the next person Tom and his spirits came to. Vic had pain in his knees and could feel a tingling feeling in his groin. But when Tom laid his hands on Vic's stomach, Vic could feel pins and needles through from the front to the back.

Tom then asked if he felt 'different' to which Vic replied, "Yes, the pain is not as bad," as Tom through his guides administered more healing.

The spirits then asked to see Michael Sagel who had never had healing before never mind heard of it.

Michael was nearly blind.

Tom's guides began healing on Michael's eyes.

Tom then asked Michael, "Can you see at all?"

"With my right eye I could see a small yellow light, then it would fade."

Michael then explained he could see grey patterns.

Tom suggested that he should come for more healing and with that Michael has since fixed up yet another healing session with Tom.

"With the miracles that have happened during that session, Tom Flynn is always welcome in my flat," said Joan Horvath who will be arranging yet another meeting with Tom and his spirit guides.

5/30/1988 above, 9/12/1988 below

Tom Flynn Can Confound Sceptics

I would like to offer this appreciation of a telephone reading given to me recently by Tom Flynn.

My wife who passed into spirit just over two years ago, speaking through Tom, for almost an hour, brought back memories to me of events in our lifetime, from the time of our first meeting each other in the 1930's until her passing into spirit.

• • • • • • • • • • • • • • •

Pain Free In Eire

Mr Tom Flynn, healer and medium was in Cork some weeks ago, (working). I had healing from him. I had a lot of pain in my back and legs for months.

Since having had healing from Mr Flynn I'm pain free, I found him to be excellent. I'm looking forward to his return visit to Ireland in October. I believe he is booked out in October.

God Bless him.

Tina Mullins, Cork, Ireland

It is fortunate that Tom provided me with a tape recording of the reading. This has given me the opportunity to examine the evidence in more detail and its accuracy amazes me.

In addition to putting me in contact with my wife, he also accurately described my position in the room in which I was sitting whilst the reading was taking place.

Furthermore, he gave me precise details of a bedroom and the exact position in that room of a photograph of my wife.

I have never met Tom Flynn, neither has Tom Flynn ever met me.

There is no way in which he could have obtained prior knowledge of any of the information which he gave me.

This reading in my estimation gave outstanding evidence of survival after death. Evidence, which even the most pronounced sceptic would find it impossible to fault.

Long may Tom continue to exercise his remarkable talents.

Anon

154

Tom Leaves Irish Eyes Smiling

Medium Tom Flynn has just returned from spending an extremely successful ten days working in Ireland, reports Lillian Mellamphy from County Cork.

There were many people comforted by Tom's spot on evidence of survival, who were delighted to receive messages from their loved ones who had passed over to the spirit world.

"Tom's first contact with the spirit world was with a young girl's grandfather. Her grandfather told Tom that her 21st birthday was coming up in three months time, and he would be there with her. The girl said she was a sceptic, but was quite amazed with the accurate message.

Ann Leary then received beautiful messages from her husband now in spirit who even praised Tom saying, 'May he continue his good work for spirit'.

Patricia Murphy heard from her mother who had passed suddenly with cancer. Tom was able to describe to Patricia how her mother had looked while she was on the earth plane and how well she looked now.

A young boy of eleven who had a problem with his legs was given spiritual healing by Tom who of course is well known not just in the British Isles and Eire but all over the world for his healing successes. The lad said he felt movements in his legs when he was receiving the healing, and was soon free of pain, much to the delight of his mother." In conclusion Lillian says, "I would like to thank Tom Flynn for coming to Ireland."

11/21/1988 above, 12/19/1988 below

Another Flynnin' Miracle!

Janet Garland from Wiltshire wanted to share with PN readers a remarkable event which took place earlier this year when she received absent healing from Tom Flynn.

It was in March this year when Janet was diagnosed with bronchopneumonia resulting in chronic laryngitis and loss of voice. She was subsequently referred by my GP to an ear, nose and throat specialist who recommended a biopsy of her left vocal chord, as it showed abnormal cells.

"As you can imagine, I was extremely upset by this news as the procedure had to be done under general anaesthetic, which poses a particular threat to me. I asked at the time of consultation if these abnormal cells could spontaneously disappear and I was told they would not.

One Sunday evening I contacted Tom when I was feeling particularly depressed and told him of my problems and asked for absent healing, which he willingly agreed to do. Within three days my voice was back to normal and to date I have not had a reoccurrence of the laryngitis.

When I attended a later ENT appointment I stated to the doctor that my throat was now healed and I had the greatest difficulty in trying to persuade them to do a laryngoscopy under local anaesthetic to confirm my opinion. Eventually they capitulated, the laryngoscopy was done, and no abnormal cells were detected. I was discharged from the hospital without further surgical intervention.

This just proves to me that absent healing really does work and also to publicly thank Tom for his help to me at a very traumatic time," said a delighted but extremely relieved Janet.

155

Tom Flynn In Canada

om Flynn, of Chesterfield, England, is a medium and healer. He spent the month of October in Vancouver, Canada, and during his visit Tom demonstrated his gifts of healing and clairvoyance.

Tom Flynn first recognized his gift of clairvoyance ten years ago at the age of 31. Four years ago, he found himself moving into the field of spirit healing and was himself quite surprised at the results. Tom credits this gift to be the presence of a Dr Joseph Eisenberg, a spirit doctor who performs etheric surgery on Tom's subjects. Dr Eisenberg, a German Jew, was a surgeon who practised medicine in New York prior to his death in the early 1960's. Five psychic artists from England have all drawn sketches of Dr Eisenberg, and all have drawn the same man.

"I'm just an ordinary man but I have been able to help people," stated Tom on his arrival in Canada. Working in conjunction with Spiritualist churches in the Vancouver area, Tom utilized his gifts and produced some miraculous results.

One of Tom's greatest joys while in Vancouver was working with young Nathan Clement, a three year old who suffered a stroke a year ago. Since the stroke, Nathan's left hand was permanently clenched shut and he was unable to use it. Nathan's hand has now relaxed to its normal state and he is regaining the use of it since his few treatments with Tom and Dr Eisenberg.

My husband George has suffered for 4 years with severe chronic pain caused by nerve damage as a result of surgery. As Tom Flynn placed his hands on his rib cage, a penetrating heat permeated through his entire chest cavity. Within minutes, the pain disappeared completely. The pain relief lasted for days - something that medical science has been unable to achieve. Subsequent treatments brought the same relief.

Jody Vajda sought Tom Flynn in order to ease chronic distress in her mouth and teeth. She fell while snow skiing years ago and her ski pole knocked her mouth prior to her landing on a sheet of ice, face first. Since this accident, her teeth would 'throb and bang' at night when she laid her head on her pillow. After two treatments, she is totally free of any discomfort.

Jody's husband Chris was so impressed with Jody's results that he asked Tom if Dr Eisenberg could remove warts. Tom wasn't certain, but was willing to give it a try. As Tom pointed his finger at the cluster of warts on Chris' hand, we watched the area redden and swell slightly before the warts began to darken to black, not unlike the effect of liquid nitrogen. The warts were completely discoloured within about 10 minutes and remained so for days. Although Chris was unable to seek Tom for a further treatment, he states that the warts are smaller than before.

Ann Phillips visited Tom hoping to improve her eyesight. After only

Medium and healer Tom Flynn

one treatment, she was thrilled to once again have peripheral vision.

Bea McCloskie had endured annoying bladder problems for years, despite three surgeries to correct the condition. One treatment and she was able to sleep through the night without waking to make trips to the loo.

Doris Prentis, Reverend of the Community Spiritualist Church, has been dealing with poor health and the aftermath of two car accidents in late 1995. Doris stated that climbing stairs was difficult and painful at best, something of a test as she has 16 stairs to climb to get to her front door. She had three treatments with Tom and Dr Eisenberg and now finds that she can climb them with greater ease and significantly less pain.

Doris' husband, Sam, sought Tom as he had not been able to bend his knees for years. After his treatment with Tom Flynn and Dr Eisenberg, he was delighted to be able to squat down to the floor.

Tom explained that Dr Eisenberg is also available for all on a daily basis, regardless of where Tom Flynn might be. At a specified time every evening, we can relax and think of Dr Eisenberg, and he will come to our assistance for a 15 minute healing.

Jeri Konkin contacted her niece, Arlene Woloshyn and suggested

Report from Tammy Vermeulen

that she try Dr Eisenberg's absent healings. Arlene had been diagnosed with stomach cancer. Having already had surgery and chemotherapy, she was ready to try something else. Arlene did this on a daily basis for months before actually meeting Tom in person.

During her 15 minute healings, she would experience tugging and pulling sensations, not unlike the sensations one feels while pregnant. Arlene was curious and unsure about this and was amazed when she had her first treatment with Tom and Dr Eisenberg, in person.

The sensations were exactly the same as during the absent healing sessions! Arlene will go for further tests in the near future and we all hope and pray that the work of Dr Eisenberg has been truly successful.

Tom's remarkable gift of clairvoyance brought comfort to many by giving them proof of the presence of their loved ones in spirit.

Many were literally 'touched' by spirit as they felt a tingling sensation in their hand long before Tom would say to them that their loved one was actually 'holding their hand'.

The action of spirit holding the hand can create these tingling sensations. Messages of love and support were given along with numerous statements given as 'proof' so that one could clearly identify the spirit presence.

These are but a few of the many miracles resulting from Tom Flynn's close relationship with the world of spirit and Dr Eisenberg. Many were truly healed with the work of these two gentlemen.

Joseph Benjamin Honoured By New Finchley Spiritualists Group

At their grand opening at the Professional Development Centre at 451 High Road, Finchley, Wednesday March 25, co founders David Hyams and Tracy Antoniou announced that, with the blessing of his life partner, wife Kitty, the new assembly would be called The Joseph Benjamin Independent Spiritualists.

80 people were present, many of whom had not been to a Spiritualist meeting place before - although quite a few had - including famous medium and healer Tom Flynn.

Like so many whose names are shining lights in the Spiritualist movement, Tom's face isn't so well known to the general public, or it seems, even a large part of the Spiritualist one!

Psychic News Editor, Lyn G de Swarte, was the demonstrating medium given the honour of launching the new North London venue, and after contacts had been happily made for a couple of visitors to the spacious hall, she approached, "The young man sitting there in the yellow shirt."

Lyn then proceeded to confirm the loving presence of his mother. Here he tells it in his own words.

"What she told me touched my heart. She came to me and told me she had my mother with her, she described what she looked like and all her characteristics when she was on the

Medium Tom Flynn with Lyn G de Swarte

earth plane. She also gave me something that, with me being a working medium myself for 11 years, has never been said before, she told me of my mother's paralysed arm and hand. She also said about books of Disney characters, which is what my sister collects.

All the evidence of knowing this and that my mother is close to me is overwhelming. It is comforting to know that we can all attend Spiritualist Churches and gain comfort and peace of mind."

In the interests of truth which we all serve the Editor would like to mention that she distinctly recollects this recipient's mother saying to him through her that he helped far too many people for nothing and that she wishes he would stop doing it so much as he never thinks of himself or his own needs.

When Lyn was told after the service by the Chair the identity of the man in the yellow shirt, that it was in fact Tom Flynn the well known philanthropic healer, that particular part of the message became crystal clear to her!

▪▪▪▪▪▪▪▪▪▪▪▪▪▪▪▪▪▪

Katz And Flynn For Charity

Psychic artist Tony Katz and medium Tom Flynn are coming together for a charity evening on Wednesday June 24 for Epping Spiritualists at Thornwood Village Hall, Wealdhall Lane, Epping which starts at 8pm at an entrance fee of £5.

Medium Tom Flynn

The event is in aid of people with learning difficulties and the proceeds raised on the night will go towards buying a holiday home.

11/22/1997, previous page

4/4/1998, above

6/20/1998

TOM ENGULFED BY TUNNEL OF LIGHT IN CANADA

Dawn Elsasser from Canada reports that healer and medium Tom Flynn recently visited Halkirk in Alberta, Canada. They took some pictures of him with her family in different areas of their village.

After they got the film developed, they found to their great amazement, one picture of Tom engulfed in a tunnel of light.

It was taken at 9pm on May 26, 1998, at the Halkirk Fire Hall. The sun was down and the only lights in the Hall were overhead fluorescent ones. There were no other lights or windows in this area.

The picture was taken from east to west, and from the mezzanine floor above, and Tom is looking directly up at Dawn

The photograph of Tom Flynn taken in the Halkirk Fire Hall

who states, "It wasn't my flash that caused it. To date we have had four opinions from different mediums who all confirmed it to be spirit."

7/4/1998

Tom Flynn In The West Country

Well loved medium Tom Flynn spent a week in the West Country before flying off to Malaysia to work for three weeks. His first demonstration was in Bath, at the Beacon of Light on the Monday evening, where one of his early contacts with the world of spirit was a young man who had committed suicide.

Medium Tom Flynn

He was known to the recipient of the message as she is his mother's best friend. Information was given regarding the water garden that he had built at his mother's house. All the particulars were accepted as good evidence of this young man's survival, as in every individual communication given that evening.

On the Wednesday evening Tom gave a very good demonstration for the Bluebell Group at Sheldan School. His first message went to a lady who he named as Margaret, as her father wanted to talk to her. Evidence was given, even of the time she had made an early morning cup of tea, and much laughter was raised when her father said that she had thought of throwing away her teapot, also that she had looked at a new one on the Thursday afternoon, two weeks before while shopping in Marks & Spencers. All this was accepted as correct. After many more such evidential messages, Tom ended on a high note with another message to 'Pauline' about what she had been doing very recently.

On the Thursday of that week Tom was appearing in Bristol at the Barton Hill Settlement - a Centre run by Mervyn and Frances Thomas. Again much proof of survival was given and his healing guide Dr Eisenberg gave healing to several members of the audience.

Private sittings were given during the stay, and one specially memorable one was to a lady who had lost her seventeen year old son in an accident. Although the equipment used to record messages had worked perfectly at all sittings previously, on this occasion the tape recorder kept switching off, so eventually it was decided not to bother but to go ahead anyway. All was fine for the first ten minutes or so when family members made themselves known - then the young son came to talk through Tom to his mother, and after a while it was noticed that the tape had switched itself on and was recording what was to the lady concerned, the most important part of the message, i.e. that from her son.

Tom Flynn's week was concluded with a weekend visit to Gloucester 1st Spiritualist Church in Brunswick Square, where a workshop was held on the Saturday afternoon and concluded with a 'Clairvoyant Evening' on the Saturday and a Divine Service on the Sunday evening.

Tom's visit was arranged by Joan Williams of Chippenham, who leads the Bluebell Group for Spiritual Awareness and Healing,

10/10/1998

Tom And Tony Go To College

Psychic artist Tony Katz and medium Tom Flynn will be demonstrating at the Arthur Findlay College on Sunday January 31 at 7pm in the Sanctuary, which promises to be a highly entertaining and enlightening evening.

"It will be the first time I have demonstrated there. As for working with Tom, we go back many years, but sadly I don't work with him much these days because he is now based in Chesterfield and I'm in North London which does make it that much more difficult," Tony told Psychic News.

Tony's work for spirit is relentless as he continues to reel off booking after booking from his jam packed 1999 diary. Here are just a few from his most immediate itinerary.

Tony was accompanied by his wife and partner Beverley, who specialises in psychometry, when he worked at Wimbledon last Tuesday; he was at Epping Spiritualist Church at Thornwood Village on Friday 29, then it was off to Sheila and Tony Taylor's Centre at the Quaker Hall, Bush Road, Wanstead this Saturday January 30, before finishing off the month at Stansted Hall.

Even February is just as busy, but Tony just lives for Spiritualism.

Thursday February 11, Tony will be demonstrating along with Beverley at The Good Shepherd Church in Stamford Hill. The start time there is 7.30pm,

Then it's Potters Bar Spiritualist Church on Friday February 23 with medium Michael Redwin.

And lastly on Saturday 25, the venue is Southall, which according to Tony is a brand new church.

"We used to demonstrate in a Southall working men's club which attracted a good 30 to 40 people, and we had very good evenings there," concluded a very busy Tony Katz.

Tony, Tom & Beverley At Stansted Hall

Psychic artist Tony Katz and his partner and wife, medium Beverly, together with medium and healer Tom Flynn, made their first ever appearance at the Arthur Findlay College on Sunday January 31 which turned out be a highly evidential evening.

The College Manager, Melvin Anthony, Chaired the event which was very well attended.

"I have to admit it was slow at first to make the links, at one stage I thought I would be left with some unclaimed portraits, until a gentlemen in the audience suddenly spoke up in an emotional voice. He said that before coming that evening he had always doubted the authenticity of psychic portraits. But on recognising two of the portraits he identified as his uncle and auntie, he is now firmly convinced that this work for spirit is genuine," Tony Katz told Psychic News.

Then a lady spoke up claiming a portrait for her friend, who was sitting beside her, but who was too emotionally touched to be able to speak herself, recognising the portrait to be that of her mother whose birthday it was that day.

1/30/1999, above

2/13/1999, left

160

WINS Appeal Event Saved By Psychic News Appeal

David Harrison is pleased to report that thanks to PN, the WINS Appeal evening at Nottingham's Clifton Leisure Centre has been salvaged in style.

The venue remains the same, but the date is now Friday May 7, and the new list of mediums are:- Bryan Gibson, psychic artist John Brett (both from Sleaford), Maureen Murnan from Northamptonshire, Marrion Belfield from Devon and local man David Harrison will be Chairing.

"Thank you to all those mediums who replied to my request to work for the WINS Appeal through Psychic News. I am most grateful", said David Harrison.

And here is a list of further events for your diary.

Saturday March 13 - A Day of Private Sittings and a Mediums Rally at West Bridgford Spiritualist Church, Central Avenue, West Bridgford, (back of Central Library), Nottingham.

Saturday March 27 at 3pm to 7pm. An afternoon of Mediumship (for a charity still to be decided) at the Winning Post Centre, Marshland Road,

Healer Tom Flynn

Thursday April 1 - An evening of Mediumship and Healing with Tom Flynn from Chesterfield to be held at Durham Spiritualist Church. 2

(Date and time to be decided) - Exeter Spiritualist Church, York Road, Exeter, Devon, EX4 6PF. A Day of Lectures and Demonstrations of various aspects of Mediumship including Healing.

Do try to get along to one of these wonderful demonstrations of mediumship if you can, as you will not only enjoy the event, but you will be contributing to not just one but many good causes who benefit from the When I Need Someone charity.

Cathy Gibb

3/6/1999 above, 3/20/1999 below

Flynn Raising Funds At Durham

Durham City Church will be host to popular medium and healer Tom Flynn for the first time.

President Valerie Pattison and Ms Mary Lowe who runs the Guild of Friends in the church have invited Tom to give an evening of clairvoyance on Thursday April 1 at 7pm this is on behalf of the 'WINS' Appeal (When I Need Someone).

"Be quick, they are limited," said President Pattison, who looks forward to what promises to be a marvellous evening at Durham City SNU Church, 2 John Street, Durham 2.

Tom Flynn Answers A Call For Help

Medium and healer Tom Flynn came to the new Southall Spiritualist Church for a visit as a guest and kindly answered a call for help from myself, the new President.

I have been suffering from a slipped disc in my lower back for the last month. My outlook was bleak and after several visits to my local GP an operation was on the cards. I have been in lots of pain and discomfort and found it hard to walk and get around. Tom said he would do some healing.

Tom's guide, Dr Eisenburg, came through and performed psychic surgery. I felt my lower back was completely numb, and after half an hour of him working, I could twist and turn, touch my toes and walk totally pain free. I have had healing many times before, for different things, but never experienced anything as nice and comforting.

Through the Psychic News I would like to thank Tom and his inspirer, Dr Eisenburg, for their great work for spirit.

Tom will be coming to our church in the near future to do a special Evening of Clairvoyance and Healing, and I hope he will help everyone as much as he helped me.

Lisa Evans,
Southall Spiritualist Church

5/22/1999

162

Tom In The West Country

Tom Flynn will be making a visit to the West Country next month. Tom completed a very successful week with the Bluebell Spiritual Awareness and Healing Group last year, but due to popular demand will be travelling even further afield this time. He will be visiting venues in Bath, Bristol, Chippenham, Cirencester, Amesbury and Weston Super Mare. At these meetings he will be demonstrating mediumship together with his healing guide, Dr Eisenberg. Tom's visit has been arranged by Joan Williams of The Bluebell Spiritual Awareness & Healing Group,

5/29/1999 above, 7/17/1999 below

Healing Seminar with Tom Flynn

Medium and Healer Tom Flynn and his friends will be holding a 'Healing Seminar' on Saturday July 24, from 1pm-6pm, at the new Southall Spiritualist Church in Hortus Road, The Green, Southall in Middlesex.

163

Tom Flynn Amid The Bluebells

Tom Flynn came in for some appreciative words from Joan Williams of the Bluebell Group in Wiltshire, after his West Country tour.

Joan told PN that Tom's demonstration of mediumship impressed many who attended at the Bath 'Beacon of Light' where she said, 'messages were given with full name in many cases.'

Tom visited Avesbury the next day, delivering 'many evidential messages,' and on the Wednesday he gave healing as well as a demonstration of clairvoyance.

Thursday it was Barton Hill Settlement's turn, a centre run by Mervyn and Frances Thomas, one of the communications that Tom gave, 'being so emotional that there was hardly a dry eye in the room,' said Joan Williams who continued; "Friday included a visit to Bill Harrison's Healing Sanctuary, where Bill was preparing for his healing weekend, and then it was on to Harmony Poynt, Weston-Super-Mare, where Tom shared the platform with popular local medium Elsie Poynton.

There was such demand for seats to see this couple together, that many people had to be turned away. As

Medium and healer Tom Flynn with a psychic portrait of his healing guide Dr Eisenburg, by Tony Katz

there were many German guests at Harmony Poynt Tom and Elsie worked with Isabel, as interpretor. Much amusement was aroused when Tom told one of their regular friends, aged 90, that he had 20 years to go yet, and later in the evening this lively gentleman showed a lot of younger ones his stamina on the dance floor, doing the twist with Elsie.

A Saturday evening service at Cirencester Church was also full to overflowing, with newcomers as well as 'regulars'.

Tom, who is of course famous for his distant healing, had a change of direction during his private sittings for enquirers over the weekend. Twice he performed what is generally termed 'psychic surgery', with Joan Williams in attendance.

Joan has experience in the development of 'trance mediumship' and Tom's main guide for healing, Dr Eisenburg, took this opportunity to increase Tom's healing brief, while relieving the sitter's back problem.

A 'psychic operation' was conducted on another recipient's throat by a Dr Chan,' Joan told PN.

Tom joined Joan's Bluebell Group for their 'annual get-together at Avesbury,' at which they send 'healing to Mother Earth,' as Joan puts it. Tom also helped raise funds by a busy day's healing on July 24 for Southall Spiritualist Church.

8/7/1999

164

Tom Flynn Sees Off Unwanted Spirit Guest

Medium Tom Flynn

Phyllis Baldry moved into her new Enfield home about three years ago.

She found that downstairs was always warm, but from the hallway to upstairs, despite the heating being on throughout the winter, it always felt extremely cold.

"In fact from almost the time we moved in, everything started going wrong including electrical appliances," confessed Phyllis, who went on to explain.

"One day I was leaning over the bath, washing my hair, when someone or something grabbed my shoulder and really dug into me. I thought it was my husband messing around, so I swung round to shout at him and tell him that it hurt. When I turned round, nobody was there. I was so frightened that I was going to call in a priest to bless my house, but then I decided to phone the medium and healer Tom Flynn, who came down to London from Chesterfield on Saturday October 2 to see what he could do.

Tom picked up the cold spots straight away at the top part of the house. We then went to the corner of the top of the stairs, which was the coldest part. Tom said some prayers and told the Spectre to leave this house, and go to the light.

All of a sudden came a very fast cloud of white mist, and a sound of a 'Whoosh' went between us and flew out of the house. It was so strong that it blew my hair as if I was standing outside on a windy day.

The experience for the past three years has been so frightening. I only wished that I had got in touch with Tom sooner, because it would have saved me not only the constant fear and upset, but having to keep replacing things.

I would like to thank Tom and his spirit helpers for coming to the rescue. I am grateful to the world of spirit."

10/16/1999

Tom Rocks On!

Ray Smith and June Smith of the Gibraltar Psychic Research Society, recently invited medium and healer Tom Flynn to the Rock.

Many famous mediums, including Gordon Higginson, Albert Best and Mary Duffy, as well as other very well known mediums, have demonstrated in both Spain and Gibraltar. But this is the first time they have asked a medium to visit that they had never seen work before.

Medium Tom Flynn

Ray told PN, "Tom did attend one or two trance demonstrations that I gave in England and we have read reports of his work in Psychic News. It gives me great pleasure to report the fact that the people here thoroughly enjoyed both his demonstration and private sittings.

The demonstration was given in our Centre that was filled to capacity and very good evidence was given to those who attended. However, I always try to have a private word with all those who have a private sitting with mediums to see whether they received any very good evidence of loved ones and friends who have passed.

Tom gave thirty one private readings, including those he gave to June, as well as to Gwen Tisch, a well-known English medium who happened to be here at the same time. In fact the demand for sittings was so great that Gwen had to help out by giving some sittings that Tom could not manage to do. In any demonstration it is always difficult to assess the accuracy of the information given to people for sometimes people may say 'Yes' to please the medium. In June's sitting, Tom gave the fact that her father had suffered with gangrene and that his name was John. June was also told that when her father passed he had a pain in the chest and found it very hard to breathe. All of this information was correct, as was other information and names that Tom gave to her.

When Tom gave a sitting to Gwen Tisch, he told her that he was hearing the name of a road called Grove Road. Tom even gave the number seven, which was quite correct.

A school teacher who came for a sitting was given the fact that there was a spirit person present between the age of thirty and forty. Once again, an accurate name was given to the sitter, enabling him to know the identity of the communicator. The sitter's favourite grandmother also came through and told the sitter that she was aware of the large amount of travelling that he had done.

The sitter was told that he had been to Canada and when Tom said 'Vancouver' the sitter replied 'that's correct.' 'You had to meet two people on the island of Vancouver – a lady and a man and they took you on another boat.' 'You were so excited that you felt you could jump into the sea,' Tom continued. 'That's all correct,' replied the sitter.

A young woman of thirty years old came to see Tom. As part of the evidence Tom gave her, she was told that her husband was present. He apparently died at the age of thirty from a heart condition. The young lady was crying, full of emotion when she came out of the sitting, convinced that her husband was somewhere still thinking of her.

Many young people came to both the demonstration and for private sittings. It would take pages to illustrate the wonderful evidence that Tom Flynn was able to give them. It is sufficient to say that everyone here looks forward to the return of Tom at some near future date.

Since I know all the people who came to both demonstration and sittings, I can say with confidence that Tom seems to be well on the way to replacing some of the wonderful mediums who now dwell in the spirit world."

10/30/1999

Psychic News

The Psychic News started out as a voice for Spiritualism. It progressed from a small tabloid newspaper to the one of the best known magazines, available online and in print, of its type. The following was written by the Psychic News staff.

Psychic News was founded in 1932 by Maurice Barbanell as an independent voice for Spiritualism. Its existence owed much to spirit guidance. Barbanell was almost 30 years old and successful in commerce. He was also a trance medium for the well-known and respected spirit teacher, Silver Birch, who had teamed up with famous Fleet Street journalist, Hannen Swaffer, to address hundreds of thousands of people on Spiritualism around the country. Top mediums, such as Estelle Roberts and Helen Hughes, were often the demonstrators at these meetings.

Impressed by the interest in these events, Swaffer's accountant, Jack Rubens, suggested the launch of a Spiritualist newspaper with which he would help financially. Barbanell and Swaffer approached Ernest Oaten, editor of Two Worlds, to see if he would bring it to London and work with them to enlarge its sphere of influence, but he did not want to leave Lancashire. So Jack suggested that Barbanell -- who had no journalistic experience -- should launch a new newspaper.

Barbanell was unsure, but that night he was having a regular sitting with Estelle Roberts, as a member of her private direct voice circle, and was astonished when her spirit guide, Red Cloud, told him that he had been told what he should do -- start a Spiritualist newspaper. To do that, Red Cloud added, he would have to abandon all his commercial activities and give his earthly life to expounding Spiritualism.

That was a big step to take and Barbanell decided to seek confirmation through a medium who was unknown to him. He booked an anonymous sitting with Kathleen Barkel at her south London home, and this provided instant proof. White Hawk, her guide, entranced her and told Barbanell that Lord Northcliffe (the famous newspaper owner) was present "because of the Spiritualist newspaper which my brother, Red Cloud, had told me about".

Barbanell did not tell Estelle Roberts about this sitting, yet at the next direct voice circle Red Cloud asked him: "Are you satisfied now that you have been to my brother, White Hawk?"

He was then given instructions from both Northcliffe and W. T. Stead, another famous journalist who was also a Spiritualist, about the new newspaper's policy, with stress being put on its independence.

168

From their earliest association, long before Psychic News was mooted, Red Cloud had called Barbanell "John the scribe". The reason for this was explained when Barbanell gave the first Arthur Findlay Memorial Lecture at Stansted Hall, Essex, in 1973:

"When I asked why I had to embark on this task, he (Red Cloud) said that in a past life I had promised to return to do so".

White Hawk told him exactly the same. "This has made me have an open mind on reincarnation, which I cannot prove," Barbanell added. "Why should Red Cloud, always so accurate in presenting survival evidence, be wrong about my having a past life?"

So Maurice Barbanell agreed to start PN with Swaffer and Rubens, each contributing a third of the start-up costs of £1,000. Swaffer changed his mind before the launch, however, concerned that his critics would accuse him of making money out of Spiritualism if the newspaper made a profit. So it started with capital of just £666 13s 4d in those predecimal days.

A little later, Red Cloud told Barbanell that he had that day sent him "the man who is to supply the money" -- a reference to the on-going need for finance as the new venture got established.

Arthur Findlay, a wealthy businessman and Spiritualism's best-known and most successful author, had called at PN's offices that day to discuss writing an article on his book, On The Edge Of The Etheric. When Barbanell told him of Red Cloud's message, Findlay agreed to invest in the newspaper. He put up £1,000.

"Lacking practical experience, our capital did not last very long," Barbanell said in his memorial lecture. "We were soon in debt. On press days I was afraid to go to the printers in case someone said there would be no PN the next week unless we had paid what was owing."

"When we discussed this financial problem with Findlay he expressed willingness to increase his shareholding to £3,175 but insisted on having voting power and control. Jack and I tried to resist, but we had no option. What I secured, even though I never had any contract as editor, was a promise from Findlay, which he kept, that there would be no editorial interference."

So why did the March 1946 edition of PN carry the following, curt announcement?

"The Directors of Psychic Press Ltd announce with regret that Mr Maurice Barbanell has resigned his editorship of PN. Mr Stuart Martin has been appointed in his place."

Barbanell did not tell the story until 27 years later, during his Stansted Hall lecture.

At the end of the Second World War he had asked Findlay what he proposed to do with his controlling shares in PN. "I thought I ought to know," Barbanell explained, "because its success was largely due to my work."

"He shocked me by saying he proposed to leave these shares to the SNU." His idea was also to bequeath Stansted Hall to the same body ... I pointed out that official newspapers had no chance of being viable. They had to follow the party line, were usually dull and thus ceased to be bought except by a few.

"I offered to buy his shares. His reply was to place a highly exaggerated figure as their value, and to say this must be provided within seven days. We parted company after I ended the year's notice I had given".

Barbanell's move out of the editorial chair was premature. It was 10 years later before Findlay passed his shares to the SNU and when he did so he published in PN his expectation that the following provisions will be respected:

- *PN is always to remain an independent newspaper and is not to be transformed into one only for the expression of Spiritualists National Union policy.*
- *To ensure this, the Board of Directors should be constituted accordingly, and the editor should not be a Spiritualists' National Union official, he is to be always free to express opinions which have the approval of the Board of Directors.*
- *The qualification of future editors must be their journalistic ability, besides their full acceptance of all that Spiritualism stands*

171

for, and their complete detachment from orthodox supernatural credal religion.

- *As orthodox supernatural religion has always been, and always will be, an enemy of Spiritualism, the duty of PN is to expose its false claims and lead the people into the knowledge derived from natural religion as expounded by Spiritualism. This has always been the policy pursued by PN during my lifetime, and I hope that it will always be maintained.*

- *If the Spiritualists' National Union, does so, it will amply fulfil the trust and confidence I have placed in its leaders who, if they continue steadfastly to the end, will some day win the people over to the knowledge of the truth of natural religion as revealed through mediumship.*

This Charter was drawn up at Stansted Hall on May 16, 1956, and left no one in any doubt that the newspaper would keep its independence. But that did not guarantee its survival. Within six years it was in difficulties. There are those who would argue that this was the inevitable result of the SNU's involvement -- it had two directors on the board who had "an overall watching brief on the company's activities". But that would be too simplistic.

172

Barbanell had a large following of loyal readers, many of whom followed him to Psychic World, which he edited for a while before taking over as editor of Two Worlds at the request of J. B. McIndoe when that newspaper -- a long-standing and respected voice of Spiritualism -- was also on the verge of floundering. He brought it to London from Manchester and it was a lively rival to PN, both being weekly tabloids.

Red Cloud and Estelle Roberts emerge again in our story when Barbanell learned of PN's difficulties. The spirit guide gave the full name of a friend of Barbanell -- who was unknown to Estelle or anyone else connected with Spiritualism at that time -- to whom he wanted to talk. When he did so, Red Cloud told him it was his task to arrange for Two Worlds and PN to be brought together as part of the spirit plan and to function as one enterprise. He agreed.

In his Arthur Findlay Memorial Lecture, Barbanell did not name the man concerned. In fact, it was Instone Bloomfield, a hotelier and businessman who helped a number of Spiritualist and parapsychological enterprises. At first his approach to those managing the newspaper was rejected but, faced with the possibility of insolvency, they eventually agreed to sell him the SNU shares in PN.

'I must say," Barbanell commented, "that Findlay was wholeheartedly in agreement that I should return to the PN editorial chair as part of this arrangement. My friend transferred the PN

shares to Two Worlds. In turn there was formed the Spiritual Truth Foundation, a registered charity, to which these shares were transferred. This ensured that no individual could ever obtain control of this newspaper. It also assured PN's future and, incidentally, that of Two Worlds where a similar arrangement was outlined."

Well, of course, times change and Two Worlds was set free from this arrangement many years ago. As for the Spiritual Truth Foundation safeguarding the newspaper's future, that is only possible for as long as there is money available to subsidize it. The charity's resources are limited and it has a number of objectives to meet. With escalating production costs and overheads it became obvious to its trustees and the directors of Psychic Press Ltd that time was running out.

Just as Findlay came to PN's rescue in its earliest days, and the Spiritual Truth Foundation stepped in when a similar crisis loomed in the 1960s, so the SNU agreed to take over responsibility for the management of Spiritualism's only weekly newspaper and to guarantee its independence in July 1995. It's strange how these events seem to follow a 30-year cycle!

The office and archives were moved to Clock Cottage, Stansted Hall, Stansted in Essex a month later, beautifully set in the grounds of The Arthur Findlay College. The offices later moved across the courtyard to The Coach House and a purpose-built

174

extension. There, PN remained and continued to be published as a newspaper -- and produced several additional yearly publications entitled The Hydesville Magazine -- until July 2010. During this time PN was served by four editors; Julie Stretton, Lyn Guest de Swarte, Tony Ortzen (returning to the editor's role) and Sue Farrow.

Following the last newspaper edition dated 24th July 2010 and a hiatus while the previous company's affairs were dealt with by a liquidator, Psychic News was purchased by the JV Trust, and has been generously and kindly supported by them since. A new company, Psychic Press Ltd, was set up and directors Sue Farrow and Paul Brett, who both previously worked on the newspaper, set about producing the title as a magazine in 2011 -- with the help of Roy Stemman in the role of chairman.

The first bi-monthly magazine was published in December 2011, and a launch party was held at The London Spiritual Mission in Pembridge Place.

The magazine remained bi-monthly until June 2013. July 2013 saw the launch of the new-look monthly Psychic News magazine that we have today. The current editor is Roy Stemman, who worked with Barbanell on PN in the 1960s.

As of March, 2017, the Psychic News is available on many newsagents' shelves in the UK, Singapore and Australia -- and can be ordered from any other newsagent in these countries. In the USA it is available from many Barnes & Noble stores, and again can be ordered if your local store doesn't currently stock it. It can be purchased at a reduced cost from most

Spiritualist Churches as well as spiritual centres and shops.

In Conclusion

Tom's original audiotapes told his story through 2006. As of the date of this book's publication, he has continued his work as a medium and spiritual healer throughout the world. He serves Spiritualist Churches, conducts demonstrations and workshops, gives interviews for all types of news media, and now spreads his wonderful message through social media.

Like all of us, Tom looks a little different than he did in 2006, but the essence of the man is exactly the same. He lives a very simple life. He loves serving at the same churches where he began so long ago. He takes part in development circles to help other people expand and enhance their spiritual gifts. And he treasures friends he's had since childhood.

Tom has achieved a stellar, international reputation as a medium and healer, but lives a life devoted to the beliefs that guided him from the beginning. Every talk he gives and every message he gives is based on his absolute faith that life continues after death. Each individual reading demonstrates the connection that remains between the living and their loved ones in the spirit world. And every time he helps someone through spiritual healing, it is a demonstration of the power of love, and the ability of spirit guides to help.

Tom's wishes everyone to know, with absolute joy and certainty, that life transcends death, and that their loved ones are there for them in spirit.

Resources

Tom Flynn

Facebook Page:

https://www.facebook.com/tom.medium?fref=ts

Sharon S. Darrow

Facebook Page:

https://www.facebook.com/sharon.darrow

Website:

http://www.sharonsdarrow.com

Spiritualist Churches named by Tom or Psychc
News articles:

Acton Spiritualist Church

Church Website:

http://spiritual-truth.co.uk/?event-venue=acton-

Spiritualist-church

Beacon of Light Church

Church Website:

http://beaconoflightenfield.co.uk

Central Spiritualist Church

Church Website:

http://www.centralSpiritualistchurch.org

Cirencester Church

Church Website:

http://www.cirencesterSpiritualistchurch.co.uk

Durham City SNU Church

Church Website:

http://www.snu.org.uk/community/churches/durha
m.html#

Edmonton Spiritualist Church

Church Website:

http://www.snu.org.uk/community/churches/edmo
nton.html

Gloucester 1st. Spiritualist Church

Church Website:

http://www.gloucesternationalSpiritualistchurch.we
beden.co.uk

Golden Gate Spiritualist Church

Church Website:

http://www.ggSpiritualistchurch.org

Southall Spiritualist Church

Church Website:

http://www.southallSpiritualists.webeden.co.uk

The Woodgreen Spiritualist Church

Church Website:

http://www.gloucesternationalSpiritualistchurch.we
beden.co.uk

Spiritualist Organizations:

National Spiritualist Association of Churches (NSAC)

This organization was formed to include all the Spiritualists of the United States of America in one general association.

Organization Website:

http://nsac.org

Spiritualist National Union (SNU)

This organization was formed to include Spiritualists and Spiritualist organizations in the United Kingdom

Organization Website:

http://www.snu.org.uk/snu/about.html

Arthur Findlay College

SNU College

College Website:

http://www.arthurfindlaycollege.org/intro/aboutuk.
html

Bluebell Spiritual Awareness and Healing Group

Group Website:

http://www.jampat.co.uk/bluebell/

Chesterfield Psychic Study Group

Group Website:

http://chesterfieldpsychicstudygroup.weebly.com

Other Miscellaneous Resources

Carnfield Hall

Website:

http://www.carnfieldhall.co.uk

David M. Baker

Website:

http://www.mediumdavidb.com

Psychic News

Spiritualist Magazine, with a downloadable pdf version available through the website, plus an interactive app version with added video content for all computers and electronic devices available from your app store or www.pocketmags.com. The magazine also has a large number of postal subscribers from all over the world.

Facebook

Page::://www.facebook.com/psychicnews/?fref=ts

Magazine website:

www.psychicnews.co.ukhttps

Twitter: (@psychicnewsmag

Lightning Source UK Ltd.
Milton Keynes UK
UKHW03f1142150418
321066UK00005B/141/P